PORTUGUESE STUDIES

VOLUME 30 NUMBER 1
2014

Founding Editor
HELDER MACEDO

Editors
FRANCISCO BETHENCOURT
JULIET PERKINS
LÚCIA SÁ
DAVID TREECE
ABDOOLKARIM VAKIL

Editorial Assistant
RICHARD CORRELL

Production Editor
GRAHAM NELSON

MODERN HUMANITIES RESEARCH ASSOCIATION

PORTUGUESE STUDIES

A peer-reviewed biannual multi-disciplinary journal devoted to research on the cultures, literatures, history and societies of the Lusophone world

International Advisory Board

Articles to be considered for publication may be on any subject within the field but must not exceed 7,500 words, and should be submitted in a form ready for publication in English, sent as an email attachment to the Editorial Assistant at richard.correll@kcl.ac.uk. Contributions whose standard of English is inadequate will be returned. Any quotations in Portuguese must be accompanied by an English translation. Submissions in Portuguese may be considered, but publication will be conditional on provision of a satisfactory translation at the author's expense. The Editorial Assistant may undertake translations on request for a reasonable charge. Text and references should conform precisely to the conventions of the *MHRA Style Guide*, 3rd edn, 2013 (978-1-78188-009-8), £6.50, US $13, €8, obtainable in print or online version from www.style.mhra.org.uk. All articles are subject to independent, anonymous peer review by experts in the field; authors receive written feedback on the editors' decision and guidance on any revisions required. *Portuguese Studies* regrets it must charge contributors for the cost of corrections in proof deemed excessive. Books for review should be sent to: Reviews Editor, *Portuguese Studies*, Dept of Spanish, Portuguese & Latin American Studies, King's College London, Virginia Woolf Building, 22 Kingsway, London WC2B 6NR, UK.

Portuguese Studies and other journals published by the MHRA may be ordered from JSTOR (http://about.jstor.org/csp). The journal is also available to individual members of the Modern Humanities Research Association in return for a composite membership subscription payable in advance. Further information about the activities of the MHRA and individual membership can be obtained from the Honorary Secretary, Dr Barbara Burns, School of Modern Languages and Cultures, University of Glasgow, Bute Gardens, Glasgow G12 8RS, or from the website at www.mhra.org.uk.

Disclaimer: Statements of fact and opinion in the content of *Portuguese Studies* are those of the respective authors and contributors and not of the journal editors or of the Modern Humanities Research Association (MHRA). MHRA makes no representation, express or implied, in respect of the accuracy of the material in this journal and cannot accept any legal responsibility or liability for any errors or omissions that may be made.

ISSN 0267–5315 (print) ISSN 2222-4270 (online) ISBN 978-1-781881-17-0
© 2014 THE MODERN HUMANITIES RESEARCH ASSOCIATION

PORTUGUESE STUDIES VOL. 30 NO. 1

CONTENTS

Preface   1

The Unmappable Sertão   5
REX P. NIELSON

A Poetry of Flesh and Bone: Miguel de Unamuno and Miguel Torga   21
ROBERT PATRICK NEWCOMB

The Mariquinhas Cycle: An Ongoing Saga of Prostitution,
Changing Values in Lisbon and Spleen for an Undefined Past   37
MICHAEL COLVIN

Acção Realista Portuguesa: An Organization of the Anti-Liberal
Right, 1923–26   47
ERNESTO CASTRO LEAL

The Integralism of Plínio Salgado: Luso-Brazilian Relations   67
LEANDRO PEREIRA GONÇALVES

The Question of the Political Organization of Catholics under the
Portuguese Authoritarian Regime: The 'Bishop of Porto Case' (1958)   94
PAULA BORGES SANTOS

Abstracts   112

Preface

For this first issue of the thirtieth volume of *Portuguese Studies*, we are pleased to welcome authors from Brazil, Portugal and the United States, who have contributed essays on cultural and historical topics, in equal measure. In the cultural field, three themes of the Lusophone imaginary ranging from the sixteenth to the twentieth centuries are explored in contrasting media: cartography, poetry, song and architecture. **Rex P. Nielson** examines the role of Portuguese cartography and the cultural imaginary of the colonial expansion in the construction of the idea of the *sertão*, the wilderness of the Brazilian interior, that territorial and cultural symbol of Otherness. **Robert Patrick Newcomb** explores the poetic trope of 'flesh and bone' and its religious implications in the work of two closely related poets of the Iberian Peninsula, Spain's Miguel de Unamuno and Portugal's Miguel Torga. **Michael Colvin** discusses the legend of the fictitious Lisbon prostitute Mariquinhas and its evolving representations in Fado ballads, in the context of the popular scenarios of Lisbon's streets and houses.

The three remaining contributions all focus on aspects of right-wing and authoritarian traditions of political theory and organizational practice across the Lusophone world. **Ernesto Castro Leal** analyses the ideological evolution and activities of Acção Realista Portuguesa, and its distinctive brand of monarchist nationalism and corporativism, in 1920s Portugal. **Leandro Pereira Gonçalves** traces the trajectory of Plínio Salgado and his role in the formation and development of the Brazilian variant of fascism, Integralism, in the following decade, taking into account important influences from its Portuguese forerunner and from *Action Française* and its perspective on contemporary Catholicism. **Paula Borges Santos** examines how, in late 1950s Portugal, a conflict between Salazar and the Bishop of Porto brought to a focus the tensions between the regime's authoritarian suppression of independent political organization and Catholic aspirations for organizational autonomy and intervention in the public arena.

Finally, we take this opportunity to note with great sadness the death, on 16 January 2014, of our colleague Patrick Chabal, a former co-Editor of this Journal. As Professor of Lusophone African Studies and more recently Professor of African History and Politics at King's College London, where he served for nearly thirty years, Patrick was a leading international scholar and teacher of Lusophone African Politics, History and Literature, the author or co-author of nine books and the editor or co-editor of seven more. Books such as his *Africa: The Politics of Suffering and Smiling* (2009) made a major impact on interdisciplinary, public and policy debates on Africa. He was an eloquent and wide-ranging theorist, and also one of the initiators and most prominent exponents of the interdisciplinary study of Lusophone African literature. His loss will be keenly felt in many spheres, in the UK and internationally.

THE EDITORS

The Unmappable Sertão

Rex P. Nielson

Brigham Young University, UT

Perhaps no region is more significant to Brazil's national identity than the vast expanse of the country's interior commonly referred to as the *sertão*.[1] Within the Brazilian imaginary, this semi-arid landscape evokes images of cattle and leather, drought and poverty, resilience and hope. In contrast to the globally oriented metropolitan centres of the country, the *sertão* has frequently symbolized Brazil at its most authentic. Yet, the *sertão* resists definition.[2] From the moment Portuguese explorers first began mapping the new continent, the *sertão* served as a foil to European knowledge by signifying precisely that which stood outside of the defining influence of Europe.

In political, economic, social and geographic terms, transplanted European society defined itself over and against the *sertão* in a process that gave rise to a stark separation between the *litoral* [the coast] and the *sertão*. This division famously gained national attention in 1902 with the publication of Euclides da Cunha's *Os Sertões*. Published only a few short years following the proclamation of the Brazilian republic (1889), *Os Sertões* challenged republican dreams of national unity by dramatically revealing that 'a unidade nacional não existia de fato' [national unity did not in fact exist].[3] Yet even as *Os Sertões* established a paradigm for studying the tensions between the centre and the periphery (the *litoral* and the *sertão*) that have permeated twentieth-century Brazilian literary, philosophical and political thought, the origins of the contemporary symbolic significations of the Brazilian *sertão* are much older. In fact, they are not Brazilian. Long before Euclides da Cunha introduced the *sertão* to Brazil's intellectual elites, Portuguese explorers and cartographers represented the *sertão* in letters and maps. In particular, Portuguese cartography from the sixteenth to eighteenth centuries already revealed the *sertão* as a unique cultural projection of the unknown that reflected Portugal's imperial ambitions. Understanding this distinctly Portuguese cartographic phenomenon not only clarifies the

[1]   I would like to thank the Center for the Study of Europe at Brigham Young University along with the Biblioteca Nacional and Fundação Luso-Americana (FLAD) in Lisbon for the generous support that made the research for this article possible.
[2]   The term *sertão* is extremely difficult to translate. Lombardi considers *sertão* to be synonymous with 'frontier, interior, backland, hinterland, or wilderness' (p. 442). See Mary Lombardi 'The Frontier in Brazilian History: An Historiographical Essay', *Pacific Historical Review*, 44.4 (1975), 437–57.
[3]   Isabel Cristina Martins Guillén, 'O sertão e a identidade nacional em Capistrano de Abreu', in *Cultura e identidade: perspectivas interdisciplinares*, ed. by Joanildo A. Burity (Rio de Janeiro: DP&A, 2002), pp. 105–20 (p. 109). Unless otherwise noted, all translations are my own.

Portuguese Studies vol. 30 no. 1 (2014), 5–20
© Modern Humanities Research Association 2014

intellectual history of the *sertão* as both region and as cultural construct of the unknown but also provides a more complete framework for considering the future of the *sertão* within Brazilian culture.

Recent dictionaries define the *sertão* primarily in geographic terms: it is a semi-arid area with scarce and irregular rainfall that experiences periods of drought lasting months or even years.[4] Today, the *sertão* is primarily identified with the Northeast of Brazil, namely the states of Bahia, Pernambuco, Paraíba, Rio Grande do Norte, Alagoas, and Ceará. In modern parlance, the derivative term *sertanejo* refers almost exclusively to the inhabitants of these states. The *sertão* thus connotes hot temperatures, aridity and interior space located in the Brazilian Northeast, far from the coast.

Apart from these geographic qualities, modern dictionaries also emphasize a significant cultural dimension of the *sertão*, namely, as a region separated from heavily populated areas. Both Bluteau (1728) and Morais Silva (1789), for example, define the *sertão* in almost identical terms as 'região, apartada do mar, & por todas as partes, metida entre terras' [a region, separated from the sea, & from all other areas, set between lands];[5] 'lugar inculto, distante das povoações ou de terrenos cultivados; terra ou povoado afastado do litoral' [an uncultivated place, distant from settlements or cultivated lands; land or settlement set back from the coast].[6] Costa and Sampaio e Melo (1987) provide a similar primary definition for the *sertão*: 'região interior, afastada da costa e distante de povoação; floresta longe da costa' [interior region, set back from the coast and far from settlements; forest far from the coast].[7] Houaiss (2003) provides the following additional meanings: '1) região agreste, afastada dos núcleos urbanos e das terras cultivadas, 2) terreno coberto de mato, afastado do litoral, 3) a terra e a povoação do interior; o interior do país, 4) qualquer região pouco povoada do interior, em especial, a zona mais seca que a caatinga, ligada ao ciclo do gado e onde permanecem tradições e costumes antigos' [1) rural region distant from urban centres and cultivated lands, 2) land covered in dense vegetation, distant from the coast, 3) lands and populations in the interior; the interior of the country, 4) any sparsely populated region of the interior, especially, the more dry zones of the brushwood, connected to cattle raising and where old traditions and customs remain].[8] These contemporary authorities all define the *sertão* not in purely geographic or topographic terms but particularly vis-à-vis populated, civilized, and coastal space. Though commonly understood to signify the dry Northeastern region of Brazil, the *sertão* is nearly always defined

[4]   Among many examples, see *Dicionário Houaiss da Língua Portuguesa*, s.v. 'sertão'.
[5]   Raphael Bluteau, *Vocabulario Portuguez & Latino* (Coimbra: Collegio das Artes da Companhia de Jesus, 1728), p. 613.
[6]   António de Morais Silva, *Grande Dicionário da Língua Portuguesa*, 10th edn (Lisbon: Editorial Confluência, 1948), vol. x, p. 125.
[7]   J. Almeida Costa and A. Sampaio e Melo, *Dicionário da Língua Portuguesa*, 6th edn (Porto: Porto Editora, 1987), p. 1520.
[8]   Antônio Houaiss, *Dicionário Houaiss da Língua Portuguesa* (Lisbon: Temas e Debates, 2003), p. 3312.

negatively — that is, as a place notable for its opposition and separation from urban life.

Some critics have suggested that *sertão* derives etymologically from *desertão* or big desert,[9] yet other linguists contest this origin.[10] While the etymology of the word remains unclear, early uses of the term both confirm modern definitions and provide further clarification. Early Portuguese mariners, explorers, and missionaries used the word *sertão* to describe the interior region of any continent, not just Brazil. For example, in *Itinerario da Terra-sancta e suas particularidades* (1593), an account of his journey to the Holy Land, the Portuguese Franciscan priest Pantaleão de Aveiro wrote concerning the city of Damascus, 'Tratando do seu presente estado, digo que é a mais nobre e populosa cidade que tenho visto, posta em sertão' [Concerning its present

---

[9] Kalina Vanderlei Silva, 'O sertão na obra de dois cronistas coloniais: a construção de uma imagem barroca (séculos XVI–XVII)', *Estudos Ibero-Americanos*, 32.2 (December 2006), 43–63.

[10] In his *Glossário crítico de dificuldades do idioma português* (Porto: Livraria Simões Lopes, 1947), Vasco Botelho de Amaral provides a thorough examination of the term and offers several etymological hypotheses, noting the *sertão*'s connotations of both interior space and hot temperatures. He states, 'À medida que se caminha para o interior das terras ultramarinas, a temperatura é natural que seja mais elevada e, a certa altura, podia haver-se confundido a ideia de sítio quente com a de sítio interior, região longe da costa' [As one travels into the interior of ultramarine lands, the temperature naturally rises and, at a certain point in time, it may be that the idea of a hot location became identified with an interior location, region far from the coast] (p. 477). He additionally offers the following postulation: 'Visto que ninguém sabe nada quanto ao mistério da palavra, já que estou em campo de hipóteses, outra hipótese formularei para origem de *sertão*: o latim *sertus*, isto é, entrelaçado, particípio de sero, entrelaçar, enredar, etc. Para isso, convém lembrar que *sertão* pode ser floresta, mata densa no interior. As terras interiores de África e Ásia muita vez se apresentavam aos Portugueses como entrelaçadas ou densas florestas virgens. Quem sabe se, por outra hipótese que também formulo, à ideia de sertão, originariamente, se ligava a ideia de mata densa e grande? *Chi lo sa?* [...] Como vimos, há quem, aliás precariamente, relacione este vocábulo com *deserto*. Não me parece. Que é um *deserto*? Propriamente, um *deserto* é sítio abandonado, pois o latim *desertus* é um particípio de *de sero*, abandonar, deixar. *Deserto* é solitário, e daí vieram as ideias de lugar inculto, silvestre. Ora, *sertão* é só deserto grande? [...] Um aspecto que devo ainda focar: é o da portuguesidade deste termo. Se é hoje mais brasileiro que português, note-se que, antes de se aplicar às grandes regiões interiores do Brasil, referiu em bocas portuguesas sítios africanos e asiáticos. Estupenda língua, a nossa! Verdadeiro documento da presença lusíada por terras de além os mares! Como não hão-de ser misteriosas muitas palavras portuguesas, se elas ainda mantêm o mistério das terras que fomos encontrar no enigma das plagas longínquas?' [Seeing that no one knows anything about the mystery of the word, and given that I have already entered the field of hypotheses, I will offer another hypothesis for the origin of *sertão*: the Latin *sertus*, that is, interwoven, the participle of *sero*, to interweave, to entangle, etc. It should be recalled that *sertão* can be forest, dense undergrowth in the interior. The interior lands of Africa and Asia often appeared to the Portuguese as interwoven or dense virgin forests. Who knows whether, by another hypothesis that I will propose, the idea of sertão, originally was tied to the idea of dense and extensive forest? *Chi lo sa?* [...] As we have seen, there are those who precariously would relate this word with the term *deserto* [desert]. I am not convinced. What is a *deserto*? Properly, a desert is an abandoned place, since the Latin *desertus* is a participle of *de sero*, to abandon, to leave. *Deserto* is solitary, and from there comes the ideas of a wild, uncultivated place. Now, is *sertão* just a big desert? [...] Another aspect I must also note is the Portuguese-ness of the term. If today it is more Brazilian than Portuguese, note that before it was used to describe the vast interior regions of Brazil, it was spoken in Portuguese mouths to describe African and Asian locations. How stupendous our language is! A true document of the Lusitanian presence in overseas lands. How could it be otherwise that so many Portuguese words are mysterious if they still maintain the mystery of lands we encountered in the enigma of faraway regions?] (pp. 480–81).

state, I will say that it is the most noble and populous city I have seen located in the *sertão*] (p. 473). Here Damascus is notable as an exception — a populated locus of civilization situated in an otherwise unpopulated landscape. Similar examples exist in early modern Portuguese travelogues from Africa,[11] India, and the Far East[12] that make reference to interior space.

Not only does the term *sertão* refer to interior lands, but early Portuguese travellers often employed the word to describe undiscovered lands. Though a Portuguese term, the word *sertão* was almost never used to describe Portugal. Instead, the concept evolved concurrently with Portugal's overseas expansion as a term to describe lands outside of Portugal and Europe and to denote unknown space. The *sertão* symbolized the unknown. Additionally, the notion of the *sertão* was rarely employed to describe island geography but rather to connote large landmasses. Portuguese explorers and missionaries who had little knowledge of a particular landscape beyond the coast could nevertheless project continental expanse by invoking the *sertão*. Pero Vaz de Caminha, for example, uses the term twice in his famous letter of 1500 describing Brazil. Similarly, Vasco da Gama speaks of the African *sertão* in his diary of 1498 (predating the discovery of Brazil) in reference to interior lands of the African continent.[13] Neither Caminha nor da Gama actually ventured far into what might now be called the *sertão*, but they both communicated their recognition of the vast interior space by naming it *sertão*. Tracing the spread of the term *sertão* in sixteenth- and seventeenth-century Portuguese letters thus provides an outline of world geography that parallels Portugal's developing perception of new continents, especially South America and Africa, during this same period.

In these early uses of the word, the *sertão* signified not only unknown interior space but even more broadly non-European, uncivilized and even barbarous human presence. Accordingly, the *sertão* did not symbolize empty interior space as much as any cultural manifestation that was outside of European knowledge, albeit located in an interior continental space. From the word's first appearance in the late fifteenth century until the nineteenth century, and perhaps even up to the present, the *sertão* has connoted not

---

[11] See the 1609 account by Frei João dos Santos regarding Ethiopia, '[...] dos principais reinos, que há no sertão do Cabo Delgado até ao Egipto' (*Ethiopia Oriental* (Lisbon: Bibliotheca de Classicos, Portuguezes, 1891), p. 27). Another pioneering missionary of the African *sertão* was Belchior da Silva, a Brahman from Goa, who travelled extensively through east Africa in 1598.

[12] The 1614 autobiography of Portuguese explorer Fernão Mendes Pinto (d. 1583) makes several references to the *sertão* in Asia (see *Peregrinação*, chap. 143). Another example comes from one of Fernão Mendes Pinto's letters, 'Tem esta terra da China dentro polo sertão muy grandes e muy espessas mõtanhas' (p. 736). See Fernão Mendes Pinto, 'Informação de algumas coisas acerca dos costumes e leis do reino da China, que um homem honrado, que lá esteve cativo seis anos, contou no colégio de Malaca ao Padre Mestre Belchior', in *Peregrinação: versão integral em português moderno, por Adolfo Casais Monteiro. Seguida das suas cartas*, 2 vols (Lisbon: Sociedade de Intercambio Cultural Luso-Brasileiro, 1953), vol. II.

[13] Fadel David Antonio Filho, 'Sobre a palavra "sertão": origens, significados e usos no Brasil (do ponto de vista da ciência geográfica)', *Ciência Geográfica*, 15.1 (January/December 2011), 84–87. Antonio Filho provides a detailed albeit brief discussion of early uses of the word *sertão* in this article.

only geographical location but also wildness, barbarity, and non-European, non-Christian culture. In the detailed account, *As Viagens do Bispo D. Frei Vitoriano Portuense à Guiné e a Cristianizão dos Reis de Bissau* (1695), Avelino Teixeira da Mota wrote of the west African *sertão*, 'Ha entre elles como entre todas as nações desta costa huns estrangeiros tambem Ethiopes, a que chamão Mandingas de huma nação do interior de Africa, os quaes feitos Missionarios do Alcoraõ, & ministros do inferno procuraõ transfundir o veneno da sua diabolica doutrina na singelesa dos naturaes' [There are among them, as there are among all the nations of this coast, strangers, also from Ethiopia, whom they call Mandingas, from an interior nation of Africa, who as Missionaries of the Koran and ministers of hell seek to spread the venom of their diabolical doctrine to the naivety of the natives] (p. 84). Here Mota's concern over the 'diabolical' evangelizing of Ethiopian Muslims underscores his perception of the simplicity of the people and lack of religion in the west African *sertão*. In Brazil, indigenous populations in the *sertão* were likewise viewed as devoid of religion though somewhat more threatening. Besides hostile indigenous groups, Portuguese explorers faced various dangers in the *sertão*, including illness, disease, lack of food, and unpredictable weather. One Portuguese sergeant major, Teotónio José Juzarte, noted while contemplating an expedition into the Brazilian *sertão* in 1769, 'daqui para baixo não há mais igrejas, nem sacramentos' [from here on there are no more churches or sacraments].[14] Here Juzarte references the long-standing Portuguese custom of seeking the church's sacraments and last rites prior to embarking into the unknown, and it is significant how he connects this tradition to the *sertão* where the authority of the church cannot not found. In effect, the *sertão* signifies what Janaína Amado designates 'aqueles espaços desconhecidos, inacessíveis, isolados, perigosos, dominados pela natureza bruta, e habitados por bárbaros, hereges, infiéis, onde não haviam chegado as benesses da religião, da civilização e da cultura' [those unknown spaces, inaccessible, isolated, dangerous, dominated by raw nature, and inhabited by barbarians, heretics, infidels, where the benefits of religion, civilization, and culture had not yet arrived].[15]

This brief consideration of the *sertão*'s etymology along with its first uses suggests several important conclusions. In geographic terms the *sertão* connotes expansive interior space, more often associated with continents rather than islands; with regards to topography the *sertão* is a region characterized by high temperatures and irregular rainfall though not necessarily desolate, desert-like conditions, given that the *sertão* can be a landscape of dense undergrowth. In what might be called socio-geographical terms, the *sertão* is an area defined by its separation from cultivated lands and populated cities, especially familiar and well-known coastal zones. Given the fact that nothing exists very far from

---

[14]   Maria Beatriz Nizza da Silva, 'A Saga dos Sertanistas', *Oceanos*, 40 (October/December 1999), 148–58 (p. 153).
[15]   Janaína Amado, 'Região, sertão, nação', *Estudos Históricos*, 8.15 (1995), 145–51 (p. 149).

the sea in Portugal, this may explain why there is no *sertão* in Portugal. For the Portuguese, to be far from the sea was momentous, disorienting, far from the familiar. Accordingly, from its earliest uses the *sertão* has symbolized the unknown and signified Otherness, that is, both landscapes and cultures outside of European knowledge and control. Consequently, and in addition to the topographic characteristics listed above, the *sertão* emerged in early writings as a European projection of barbarous, savage, non-Christian culture.

Because maps are visual representations of space, Portugal's rich cartographic tradition has contributed significantly to the ways in which the *sertão* has been imagined. As Christian Jacob argues, 'The map is what allows a mental schema to be concretized, objectified, and reproduced, with corrections, additions, and commentary. [...] The map reconstructs the space it represents, organizing it and optimizing its legibility and visibility.'[16] Jacob's summary emphasizes the interpretive quality of maps. Maps provide navigational assistance, yet they rarely represent space in an innocent manner. As symbolic representations of the world, maps frequently bear the signs of calculated political and economic desire. As Linda Hutcheon, Djelal Kadir, and Mario J. Valdés note, 'Societies produce space as "territory," as a manifestation of culture. In seeking to map such territory, [we must] be aware of the less than innocent nature of cartography and, indeed, of geography. Mapping has always been a way to make something exist for imperial eyes.'[17] Thus, more than merely satisfying 'the desire for symbolic mastery of the world',[18] maps serve important administrative functions: 'ruling over a province, a nation, a kingdom, an empire, protecting or conquering a territory, imposing upon it the rationality of an administrative grid, a political project of reform or of development.'[19] Accordingly, maps operate as important tools for power.

The *sertão* symbolizes a concept that resists the epistemological power and effect of maps. As a Portuguese symbol for the unknown, for that which stood outside of European knowledge, the *sertão* maintained an elusive presence in early modern maps. In a sense, the *sertão* paradoxically represented a space that could not be mapped. To map, that is, to locate the *sertão* within the rationality of the epistemological grid of European knowledge would be to endow the *sertão* with qualities that contradict its very definition as a sign for the unknown. As such, the *sertão* emerges as an uneasy, unstable, and even fluid sign within early modern Portuguese cartography. The *sertão* shifts locations from one map to another and moves easily, always resting just beyond the grasp of cartographic knowledge. This fact should not be interpreted as evidence of a failing or inconsistency of cartographic skill, but rather as a result of the *sertão*'s

---

[16] Christian Jacob, *The Sovereign Map: Theoretical Approaches in Cartography throughout History* (Chicago, IL: University of Chicago Press, 2006), p. 28.
[17] Linda Hutcheon, Djelal Kadir, and Mario J. Valdés, *Collaborative Historiography: A Comparative Literary History of Latin America*, Occasional Papers 35 (New York: American Council of Learned Societies, 1996), p. 2.
[18] Jacob, p. 66.
[19] Jacob, p. xviii.

conceptual essence. How could it be otherwise? The *sertão* is a sign that resists the symbolic order.

The unique nature of this Portuguese sign thus reveals the limits of European knowledge and how those limits change over time. Given that maps represent territory, dominion, law, and order, the presence of the *sertão* in cartography provides insights into the Portuguese conception of space as the Portuguese empire eyed the new lands entering European knowledge. Luís Adão da Fonseca has eloquently discussed the transformation in the Portuguese conception of nautical space and the evolution of oceanic space that occurred in the fourteenth and fifteenth centuries, as Portuguese explorers moved beyond the closed space of the Mediterranean Sea and coasts of Europe into the unknown space of the ocean. Fonseca argues, 'o Oceano surge como o que está para *além do mundo*; de facto, está *para além da terra*, porque está fora do espaço habitável. É o espaço do desconhecido que está para além das fronteiras do mundo conhecido, onde se desenha o horizonte do inabitável, entendido como espaço do não-humano. Em última análise, é o *selvagem* e o *incomensurável*' [the Ocean emerges as that which is *beyond the world*; in fact, it is *beyond the land*, because it is outside inhabitable space. It is the space of the unknown that is beyond the frontiers of the known world, where the horizon of the uninhabitable is drawn, understood as an inhuman space. In sum, it is *savage* and *immeasurable*].[20] In a parallel manner, the *sertão* signifies *what lies beyond* the known world in revealing the continental expanse of newly discovered lands.

One of the earliest known maps representing Brazil and South America, the Cantino planisphere of 1502, accurately depicts the outline of Africa and includes a rough contour of the northeast coast of Brazil.[21] Little was known of Brazil at this point, yet the map contains a small but beautiful landscape painting situated along the Brazilian coast. The green landscape scene features three striking red macaws with blue tails. Behind them stands a line of trees, and behind the trees a swath of blue, perhaps a river or a lake in reference to Caminha's description of the new land's many waters. Behind the waters extends only blank space. Yet this blank space is not entirely empty. Though devoid of topographical features of any kind, the map's rhumb lines — the lines projecting navigational bearings relative to compass directions — extend into this space.

[20] Luís Adão da Fonseca, 'O horizonte insular na experiência cultural da primeira expansão portuguesa', in *Portos, escalas e ilhéus no relacionamento entre o ocidente e o oriente: actas do congresso internacional comemorativo do regresso de Vasco da Gama a Portugal*, ed. by Avelino de Freitas de Meneses, 2 vols (Lisbon: Comissão Nacional para as Comemorações dos Descobrimentos Portugueses, Universidade dos Açores, 2001), I, 55–93 (p. 57).
[21] The earliest known map to represent the Brazilian coastline is currently thought to be the 1500 map made by Juan de la Cosa, who sailed on Columbus's first and second voyages, though the representation of Brazil appears to be conjectural in nature. See John Noble Wilford, *The Mapmakers* (New York: Vintage, 2000), p. 80. The Cantino map is significant as the first map to accurately represent Brazil's coastline and latitude. For an excellent technical discussion of the Cantino map, see Joaquim Alves Gaspar, 'From the Portolan Chart of the Mediterranean to the Latitude Chart of the Atlantic: Cartometric Analysis and Modeling' (unpublished PhD dissertation, Universidade Nova de Lisboa, 2010), p. 129.

In fact, deep in the interior space of this new continent sits a compass rose with sixteen intersecting rhumb lines on the Tropic of Capricorn. The rhumb lines clearly show the direction from Africa to Brazil, thereby establishing a direct connection to Portugal and Europe, that is, the rhumb line indicates the actual path to the New World. (Rhumb lines in Portuguese are called *rumos*, literally 'paths'). In similar fashion, the landscape of the new continent is also overlaid with rhumb lines. These lines operate an important transformation by which land becomes territory. The map incorporates the unknown geography of the new continent into Europe's intellectual and political dominion.

Though the Cantino map does not explicitly reference the *sertão*, it is an important early example of how European cartography generally speaking, and Portuguese cartography specifically, dealt with the New World's unknown space.[22] Perhaps to compensate for the lack of topographical and geographical information, the map includes not only a landscape illustration but also two written notes, which appear on the map alongside Brazil's coast. The first states that although the explorers did not land, they observed thick mountain ranges, and that the land is believed to be the edge of Asia.[23] The second note offers this description of the land: 'a qual terra se cree ser terra firme em a qual a muyta gente de descricam andam nuos omes e molheres como suas mais os pario sam mais brancos que bacos e teem os cabellos muyto corredios' [this land here, which is believed to be a continent, in which there are many people who go about naked as their mothers delivered them; they are more white than brown and have very lanky hair].[24] Though the map includes only a partial

---

[22]   Duarte Leite has convincingly shown that the Cantino planisphere is of Portuguese origin and not Italian, and Armando Cortesão and Avelino Teixeira da Mota dedicate several paragraphs to the map's provenance in their *Portugaliae Monumenta Cartographica*, 5 vols (Lisbon: Imprensa Nacional–Casa da Moeda, 1960), which was published as part of the Comemorações do V Centenário da Morte do Infante D. Henrique. The map was initially owned by Alberto Cantino, the secret agent of Ercole d'Éste, the Duke of Ferrara, who was sent to Portugal to acquire Portuguese nautical information.

[23]   The original text reads: 'Esta terra he descober per mandado muy escelentissimo pncipe Dom manuel Rey de portugall a quall se cree ser esta a ponta dasia E os que a descobriram nam chegarõ a terra mais vironla nam virom senam serras muyto espessas polla quall segum a opiniom dos cosmofricos se cree ser a ponta dasia' [This land is discovered by order of the very excellent prince Dom Manuel King of Portugal, which is believed to be the point of Asia, and those who discovered it did not land, but saw it, and only saw mountain ranges very thick, and according to the opinion of the cosmographers it is believed to be the point of Asia] (Cortesão and Mota, p. 11; translation by Cortesão and Mota).

[24]   The complete text of the second note reads: 'a vera cruz ✠ chamada p. nome a quall achou pedraluares cabrall fidalgo da cassa del Rey de portugall τ elle a descobrio indo por capitamoor de quatorze naos que o ditto Rey mandaua a caliqut e enel camjnho indo topou com esta terra em a qual terra se cree ser terra firme em a qual a muyta gente de descricam andam nuos omes τ molheres como suas mais os pario sam mais brancos que bacos τ teem os cabellos muyto corredios foy descoberta esta dita terra em a era de quinhentos' [The True Cross ✠, called by this name, which was found by Pedro Alvares Cabral, a nobleman of the house of the King of Portugal, and he discovered it when he went as captain-major of fourteen ships which the said King was sending to Calicut and going this way he met with this land here, which is believed to be a continent, in which there are many people who go about naked as their mothers delivered them; they are more white than brown and have very lanky hair. This said land was discovered in the year five hundred] (Cortesão and Mota, p. 11; translation by Cortesão and Mota).

outline of Brazil, the note suggests the continental dimension of the new land. Together, the landscape illustration and verbal description supplement the lack of cartographic knowledge.

Other notable examples from sixteenth-century cartography that represent the interior of Brazil as blank space include Diogo Ribeiro's 1529 atlas, Pedro Reinel's 1535 and 1540 maps, Gaspar Viegas's 1534 map, and Lopo Homem's 1554 *mappa mundi*. This blank interior space did not remain empty for long, however. Almost immediately, Europeans began to project both desire and fear onto the empty expanse of the unknown continent. As early as 1519, Lopo Homem's map, commonly referred to as the Miller Atlas, appears as a remarkable example of such European imaginings. In this map, the Brazilian interior is filled with thick and red woods, exotic, multi-coloured birds and animals (even dragons!), and indigenous figures. Despite having no reliable information on the actual people or landscape of the continent's interior, maps from this period present the interior of Brazil as a natural paradise filled with wealth and natural resources like Brazil wood (see also Diogo Ribeiro's map of 1532). Yet there are just as many examples, like Diogo Homem's 1558 map, that fill the so-called 'terra incognita' / 'regio incognito' with threatening scenes of cannibalism and hostile natives. This map shows graphic images of natives shooting bows and arrows and holding other weapons, and also cooking human body parts, including legs and arms, and hanging them on the branches of trees.

Perhaps the first map to explicitly reference the *sertão* is found in the anonymous *Roteiro de todos os sinaes conhecimentos, fundos, baixios, Alturas e derrotas que ha na Costa do Brasil desde Cabo de Sãto Agostinho até o estreito de Fernão de Magalhães* (*c.* 1590). Armando Cortesão attributes this atlas to the cartographer Luís Teixeira, one of Portugal's foremost mapmakers of the sixteenth century, known for his elegant style and use of colour.[25] The map in question is a general map of Brazil and not only shows the demarcation line established by the Treaty of Tordesillas (1494) but also clearly indicates the boundaries of the colonial captaincies (jurisdictional divisions analogous to a province).[26] The map shows Brazil's major rivers but no other topographical features. The map includes, however, a large inset box, positioned in the upper-left corner of the map, above the Tropic of Capricorn, that contains a lengthy verbal description of Brazil with the following comment:

> tem cada huã destas capitanias pella costa do mar 50 léguas e pera o Sertão, tanto ate chegar a linha da demarcacam como na repartição dellas se ve. he povoada esta terra do Brasil toda de portugueses quãto dizem as Capitanias e somente ha costa do mar e quãdo muito 15, 20 léguas pello Sertão he muy

---

[25] Cortesão, p. 49. Joaquim Romero Magalhães attributes this map as well to Luís Texeira in his article 'O reconhecimento da costa', *Oceanos*, 39 (1999), 102–12. Alfredo Pinheiro Marques does the same in 'A cartografia do Brasil no século XVI', *Revista da Universidade de Coimbra*, 34 (1998), 447–62.
[26] Most of the original *capitanias* [captaincies] eventually evolved into provinces and states, though with significant changes to their territorial boundaries, during the nation-building period of the late nineteenth and early twentieth centuries.

povoada do gentio da terra tem muytos mãtimentos, em partes della há
Ouro. assi de Minas

[each of these captaincies extends along the coast 50 leagues and into
the Sertão, until reaching the demarcation line as can be seen in their
distribution. The Portuguese have settled this land of Brazil in terms of the
Captaincies and only along the coast, and at most 15, 20 leagues into the
Sertão, there are many native settlements with many provisions, in parts of
them there is Gold, as well as Mines]

Despite the limited knowledge of Brazil available at the time, the map's written
description posits the convenience of wealth deep in the *sertão*. Visually, the
captaincy lines on the map overlay the interior of the country, referred to in its
entirety as *sertão*. These lines symbolize the Portuguese appropriation of the
region. As a symbolic projection of law and order with clearly defined borders
and limits, the captaincy's demarcation on the map demonstrates universal
dominion.[27] Notably, the word *sertão* — an indication of space and culture
outside of Portuguese control — does not appear on the map itself but only in
the verbal description. Thus, without explicitly locating the *sertão* on the map
using cartographic signs, the map nevertheless acknowledges the presence of
the *sertão*, that is, the limits of Portugal's knowledge of the Brazilian interior.
The verbal description, which tacitly concedes the constraints of Portugal's
authority over the land, thus works against the visual symbols, which express
political authority over the territory.

In the seventeenth century, the term *sertão* begins to appear with greater
frequency on Portuguese maps, though it does so in distinctive ways.[28] For
example, the word appears on several maps in the 1631 Atlas of Brazil made by
João Teixeira Albernaz I, son of Luís Teixeira and a prolific mapmaker in his
own right. Throughout the 1631 Atlas, the term *sertão* is used only in reference
to the territory of indigenous populations, such as on the map detailing the
mouth of the Amazon River, which includes the following place names: 'sertão
dos Tupiãbas', 'sertão dos Tocantins', 'sertão dos Pirapes', 'sertão dos Tacares',
and 'sertão dos Tapuyossus'. Here, the use of the word *sertão* underscores the
cultural Otherness of these non-European indigenous groups. Rather than
merely leave the interior of the land as white space, the maps identify the
homelands of various indigenous tribes, yet it is significant that tribal lands are
not separated on the map by political boundary lines as the captaincies are in
Luís Teixeira's *c.* 1590 map. Instead, the place names float in the interior blank
space of the map, suggesting both Portugal's lack of political and administrative
oversight of these areas as well as general lack of knowledge regarding the
frontiers of its territories.

[27] For an interesting point of comparison, see John Mitchell's 1755 *Map of the British and French
Dominions in North America* (held in the Newberry Library) or John Blair's 1768 *Map of the North
American Colonies*. In both of these maps, the lines of the original colonies extend westward all the way
to the Mississippi River in the same fashion as the captaincy lines on Luís Teixeira's map.
[28] It should be noted that being a uniquely Portuguese term, the word *sertão* never appears on
Spanish, French, British, or other non-Portuguese maps.

A decade later, in 1640, João Teixeira Albernaz I produced another Atlas of
Brazil with almost identical individual maps, though with some notable differences. Like the 1631 Atlas, the map of the mouth of the Amazon River continues
to identify the territories of indigenous tribes, though this map replaces the term
sertão with *província* [province] as follows: 'Provincia dos Tocantins', 'Provincia
dos Tupinabas', 'Provincia dos Pirapes', 'Provincia dos Tacares', 'Provincia dos
Tapuyossus'. The change from *sertão* to *província* suggests a significant shift in
how Portugal viewed these lands. More than merely acknowledging the presence
of indigenous groups in particular areas, the 1640 Atlas appears to reflect
Portugal's increased knowledge of these areas by recognizing the autonomy
and perhaps even the political organization of local indigenous populations.[29]
This phenomenon manifests itself on several seventeenth-century maps where
a particular mapmaker replaces the term *sertão* on subsequent maps of the
same area with terms such as *província* or *serra*. João Teixeira Albernaz I,
for example, produced at least three major atlases of Brazil over the course of
three decades, and his later maps demonstrate a clear preference for the terms
província and *serra* over *sertão* to denote interior space.[30]
    Towards the end of the seventeenth century and then in the eighteenth
century the word *sertão* appears less and less in atlases and general maps of
Brazil. Two hypotheses may explain this. First, as the Portuguese captaincies
became more firmly established and as explorers and missionaries ventured
further and further into the unknown frontier, Portuguese geographical
knowledge increased and maps became progressively detailed in representing
scales, rose compasses, gradations, etc. If the *sertão* cartographically signals
unknown space, then it follows that the word would gradually disappear from
Portuguese maps as geographic knowledge increased.
    A second circumstance may also explain the disappearance of the *sertão*
from general maps of Brazil from this period, namely the tensions between
Spain and Portugal leading up to the 1750 Treaty of Madrid. Disagreements over
the boundaries between Spanish and Portuguese territories increased during
the early 1700s and eventually resulted in several joint Luso-Hispanic mapping
expeditions. The Portuguese crown nominated Alexandre Gusmão to help lead
the boundary negotiations, and he assumed responsibility for producing the
well-known *Mapa das Cortes* in 1749. Gusmão made Portuguese and Spanish

---

[29] This change may possibly be a result of new knowledge resulting from the 1637–39 expedition led by
Pedro Teixeira to acquire more information about the Amazon region. Unfortunately we do not know
of any connection between Pedro Teixeira and João Teixeira Albernaz, or whether the cartographer
João Teixeira Albernaz even had access to the information resulting from Pedro Teixeira's expedition.
Nevertheless, the impact of Pedro Teixeira's exploration of the Amazon was extensive and has been
well documented by historians such as Iris Kantor and Jaime Cortesão. See, for example, Jaime
Cortesão, 'O significado da expedição de Pedro Teixeira à luz de novos documentos', in *Anais do IV
Congresso de História Nacional* (Rio de Janeiro: IHGB/IBGE, 1950), vol. III, pp. 188–94.
[30] Both João Teixeira Albernaz's 1631 Atlas of Brazil and his 1640 Atlas of Brazil include a detailed
map of the captaincy of São Vicente and the 'destricto do Rio de Ianeiro'. The interior space of these
two maps is filled with place names that use the term *serra*, e.g., 'Serra de Saranapíacaua', 'Serra
Piratininga', 'Serra de Maricara', 'Serra de de Mariaitiba', etc.

versions of this map, which served as the foundational text for re-establishing the border between Spanish and Portuguese territories in South America. The *Mapa das Cortes*, subtitled in Portuguese *Mapa dos confins do Brazil com as terras da Espanha na America Meridional*,[31] does not include any reference to the *sertão*. Nevertheless, if the word *sertão* had the symbolic function of unknown and, more significantly, land outside of Portuguese administrative control, then it would have been in the interest of the Portuguese to avoid using the term on official maps in an effort to show as much control over the interior of the continent as possible.

A similar effect occurs in the maps created in preparation for the 1777 Treaty of San Ildefonso, which again realigned the boundaries between Spanish America and Portuguese America by granting Portugal authority over the Amazon River basin and Spain control over what is now the area of Uruguay. Concerning the maps made in preparation for this treaty, Manuel Lucena Giraldo notes:

> Algumas regiões marginais e quase desconhecidas transformam-se em menos de quatro décadas em domínios de grande valor estratégico, com uma rede de povoações de grande solidez e com uma economia em expansão. As expedições de limites [...] foram o agente fundamental dessa transformação, na qual se configura o mundo selvático *moderno* e se criam as bases de um processo de *descoberta*, de produção de espaço ocidentalizado.[32]

> [In less than four decades, some marginal and nearly unknown regions are transformed into territories of great strategic value, with a network of established settlements with an expanding economy. The border expeditions [...] were a fundamental agent in this transformation, in which the *modern* forest world is configured and bases are established for a process of *discovery*, for the production of western space.]

The royal mapping expeditions associated with the 1750 Treaty of Madrid and the 1777 Treaty of San Ildefonso not only established the triangular contour of Brazil but reconfigured the Brazilian landscape as a territory fully under Portuguese dominion. Furthermore, by not including any reference to the *sertão* or any other indigenous group — i.e., by avoiding the signs and symbols of the unknown — maps like the *Mapa das Cortes* authoritatively claimed the area of Brazil as *espaço ocidentalizado*, that is, as Portuguese territory ready to be exploited.

Though the term *sertão* disappeared from general maps of Brazil during the eighteenth century, it nevertheless remained present on numerous maps of a more limited scope related to the exploration of the Brazilian interior. Such exploration was motivated by a desire to fend off competing Spanish incursions

---

[31]   In the Spanish version of the map, the *Mapa de las Cortes* included the subtitle *Mapa de los Confines del Brazil con las tierras de la Corona de Esp^a en la America Meridional*. See Synésio Sampaio Góes, 'Alexandre de Gusmão e o Tratado de Madrid', *Oceanos*, 40 (1999), 45–62 (p. 57).

[32]   Manuel Lucena Giraldo, 'Reformar as florestas: o Tratado de 1777 e as demarcações entre a América espanhola e a América portuguesa', *Oceanos*, 40 (1999), 66–76 (pp. 75–76).

into the interior of the continent but also by Portugal's own desire to understand the available resources of its territories. In a royal letter of instruction dated 18 November 1729, Dom João V ordered: 'convem muito que se façaõ mapas o mais que for possível dos vastos certões do mesmo Estado, especialmente nos da Minas' [it is very desirable that maps be made as far as possible of the vast *sertões* of the same State, especially in those of Minas].[33] Numerous maps date from this period, showing various routes of entry into the Brazilian interior, and these routes can be grouped into two types: 1) routes entering the *sertão* by canoe, and 2) overland routes by horse or mule. The first maps predominantly represent fluvial networks. For example, the eighteenth-century map *Exemplo Geografico e descrição demonstrativa das terras e rios mais principaes* clearly shows the primary rivers that provided access into the *sertão*. This map, which focuses on the 'Capitania de Goyas', shows rivers in detail. Blank space borders the river network and is filled with the following designations: 'Certão dos Aycurús ou Cavalleiros', 'Certão Bororós', 'Campos da Vacaria', 'Reino do Gentio Caypó'. Notably, the lands further west, that is, further into the frontier are labelled *certão* (an archaic variant spelling of *sertão*), while the lands on the east side of the map are called 'Campos' or 'Reino' — suggesting on the one hand that the land is a natural resource, in this case for cattle raising, and on the other hand acknowledging the social organization of the Caypó people. Here again, the *sertão* is linked with unknown indigenous presence rather than topographical features.[34]

Another notable map that references the *sertão* in a similar way is the *Carta Topografica em q'. se observam os lemites, e extensão da Cap.^{ta} de Matto Groço a mais Ocedental d'America Portugueza* (1773).[35] As the title indicates, this map represents the westernmost territory of Portuguese America. While primarily showing the captaincy of Mato Grosso, the map also includes portions of the captaincy of Pará and the captaincy of Goiás. Situated in the frontier regions of the map are two designations written in large font 'terras incognitas'. Within these 'terras incognitas' are located numerous indigenous groups: 'certão do gentio muras', 'certão do gentio acruá', 'certão do gentio cayapo'. By visually overlaying the various indigenous groups with the term 'terras incognitas', this map explicitly links the unknown with the *sertão*. A similar example is the *Mapa da freguesia da Manga* (1764).[36] This map of the parish of Manga in Minas Gerais unsurprisingly shows the location of various chapels and churches, as well as numerous rivers. The population centres are all located along the river network, and separate from these various settlements lies an area designated as 'Sertão Povoado de Gentio Cómição' [*sic*]. This label indicates the missionary

---

[33] Jaime Cortesão, *História do Brasil nos velhos mapas* (Rio de Janeiro: Instituto Rio Branco, 1971), p. 215.
[34] Nizza da Silva, p. 151.
[35] See *Cartografia da conquista do território das Minas*, ed. by Antônio Gilberto Costa (Belo Horizonte: Editora UFMG, 2004), p. 35.
[36] See Costa, p. 20.

efforts of the parish with regards to an indigenous group (*Gentio Cómição* literally meaning *gentio com missão* or natives with missionaries present). Once more the term *sertão* signifies non-Christian and ethnic otherness rather than geography.

Over the course of the eighteenth century, Portuguese maps reference the *sertão* not only to project cultural otherness but also to suggest the location of valuable natural resources. This occurred on maps as early as the Cantino planisphere where the interior of Brazil was filled with illustrations of rich forests of Brazil wood; however, the *sertão* is specifically linked to precious metals in the eighteenth century, following the discovery of significant amounts of gold as well as imperial topaz, iron ore, tourmaline and diamonds in Minas Gerais in the late seventeenth century and early eighteenth century. Accordingly, eighteenth-century cartography frequently appropriates the *sertão* as a symbol for the unknown and inscribes it with European fantasies of wealth. One example of such an inscription is the *Carta Topographica das Terras entremeyas do sertão e destrito do Serro do Frio com as novas minas dos diamantes*, offered to Cardeal da Mota by Jozeph Rodrigues de Oliveyra in 1731.[37] This map shows the locations and overland routes to various settlements situated at known diamond mines in the interior of what is now Minas Gerais. Apart from these known mines, the map identifies two separate areas of 'sertoes despovoados' [unpopulated *sertões*] where 'descubrim das esmeraldas' [emeralds can be found]. Rather than identifying the location of known emerald mines, similar to the diamond mines, the map projects emeralds into the unknown space of the *sertão*. Another example that illustrates this well is the *Mapa da região banhada pelo Rio Doce e seus afluentes na Capitania de Minas Gerais (c. 1750)*.[38] Like the *Carta Topographica das Terras entremeyas do sertão*, this map includes a detailed representation of the paths leading into the *sertão* — in this case via the Rio Doce. On the right-hand side of the map, separate from the river network, the mapmaker has drawn a three-dimensional illustration of a mountain range. On the far side of the mountain range is written: 'Minas novas' [New mines]. On the near side, closer to the river system, the map states: 'Campos das Esmeraldas com varios montes e por descobrir' [Emerald fields with various mounts yet to be discovered]. As in the diamond map listed above, this map acknowledges the limits of Portuguese information about the interior of the land while projecting natural wealth into the *what lies beyond* symbolized by the *sertão*.

The discovery of extensive deposits of gold in the 1690s, and of diamonds and other precious stones in the 1720s, led to a significant migration into the *sertão* that continued throughout much of the eighteenth century.[39] As Portuguese

---

[37] See Costa, p. 54.
[38] See Costa, p. 71.
[39] This well-documented phenomenon has received extensive analysis by historians, cultural anthropologists and sociologists. Among many examples, see Antonio Carlos Robert Moraes, *Território e história no Brasil* (São Paulo: Annablume, 2005); Silvia Maria Jardim Brügger, *Minas*

settlements in the *sertão* grew, so too did the need for administrative supervision. Resentment over increased Portuguese colonial oversight consequently resulted in various forms of social and political unrest in the *sertão*, the most famous case being the *Inconfidência* or 'Conspiracy' of 1788–89. Writing about this generally turbulent period and the expansion of governmental institutions in the *sertão*, Luciano Figueiredo notes, 'A pacificação e a redução do sertão dependeu também da montagem de um aparato administrativo da justiça para atender àquelas populações' [The pacification and reduction of the sertão depended also upon the establishment of a legal administrative apparatus in order to serve those populations].[40] Figueiredo's choice of words here is revealing: the presence of administrative entities led not only to an increased government presence and expanded legal culture but also to a reduction of the *sertão*. In other words, as the colonial administrative apparatus increased, the *sertão* — symbol of lands existing outside of Portuguese control — likewise diminished and literally disappeared as a place marker in legal discourse.

By the nineteenth century, references to the *sertão* all but disappear from official cartography. Following Brazil's independence in 1822, Dom Pedro I promoted a variety of scientific expeditions to explore, map, study, observe, and otherwise report on the still-unknown regions of the Brazilian interior. These scientific missions systematically surveyed the Brazilian interior and clarified the cartographic understanding of Brazil's territory. Unsurprisingly, the *sertão* as a marker for unknown space makes no appearance on these maps. Nevertheless, the *sertão* remained a potent symbol for the unknown in other writings. For example, Karl F. P. von Martius participated in one such expedition and subsequently wrote his now-famous essay, 'Como se deve escrever a história do Brasil' (1843).[41] In this essay, von Martius perceptively analyses key elements of Brazil's history, yet he also acknowledges continued lack of scientific and historical knowledge of the *sertão*, which he asserts should be better known.[42]

One final map worth mentioning is the *Atlas do Império do Brasil*, prepared by Cândido Mendes Almeida and presented to the emperor, Dom Pedro II, in 1868. By this point in history, the modern cartographic image of Brazil is well defined; the only ambiguous areas are located in Amazonia and Mato Grosso, the same areas that on earlier maps were so frequently identified as *sertão*. Almeida's Atlas includes individual maps of each of Brazil's provinces as well as a general map of Brazil showing all of the provinces. Throughout the atlas,

---

patriarcal: família e sociedade (São João del Rei — Séculos XVIII e XIX) (São Paulo: Annablume, 2007); Marcia Amantino, *O mundo das feras: os moradores do sertão oeste de Minas Gerais — Século XVIII* (São Paulo: Annablume, 2008).

[40] Luciano Figueiredo, 'Furores sertanejos na América portuguesa: rebelião e cultura política no sertão do rio São Francisco, Minas Gerais (1736)', *Oceanos*, 40 (1999), 128–44 (p. 140).

[41] Karl Friedrich von Martius and José Honório Rodrigues, 'Como se deve escrever a Historia do Brasil', *Revista de Historia de América*, 42 (1956), 433–58.

[42] Lombardi, 'The Frontier in Brazilian History', p. 444.

maps of individual provinces identify various unpopulated areas of the country, yet for the most part, these unpopulated areas are merely left blank, or they are given descriptive names regarding their use. For example, on the map of the 'Província de Sergipe', the blank unpopulated interior space of the province is designated as 'Campos de criação de gados' [Fields for raising cattle]. Throughout the atlas, the term *sertão* remains absent, except for one notable exception. On the map of the 'Província de Espírito Santo', the unpopulated space north of the Rio Doce and south of the Rio S. Matheus in Bahia is designated in large print as 'Sertão Desconhecido'. Interestingly, the map shows the location of two separate indigenous groups: 1) 'Indigenas Botocudos' and 2) 'Indigenas Prokane e Batata'. Here the term *sertão* does not signify indigenous otherness but nonetheless identifies a remote area of the interior of Bahia. Significantly, this official map of the Brazilian empire locates what appears to be the last remaining outpost of the unknown not in Mato Grosso or the Amazonian border regions contested by Bolivia and Peru but rather in Bahia. This is significant because two decades following the creation of Almeida's map, the Bahian *sertão* would serve as the location for the traumatic conflict at Canudos, which Euclides da Cunha documents in *Os Sertões*. And given the cartographic tradition of the *sertão*, it is not inconsequential that Euclides da Cunha subtitles the first part of *Os Sertões* 'terra ignota'.

Thus, while da Cunha's *Os Sertões* established a twentieth-century model for considering the strains between *litoral* and *sertão*, the centre and the periphery, the cartographic record demonstrates that the conceptual origins of the *sertão* begin much earlier. As Kalina Silva succinctly states, 'A ideia de sertão existia no imaginário desde o século XVI, construída a partir de uma oposição entre as regiões colonizadas no litoral da América portuguesa e aquelas não inseridas na jurisdição metropolitana' [The idea of the *sertão* existed in the [Brazilian] imaginary since the sixteenth century, constructed on the basis of an opposition between the colonized coastal regions of Portuguese America and those outside of the metropolitan jurisdiction].[43] Portuguese cartography from the sixteenth to the eighteenth century endowed the *sertão* with symbolic power to project the unknown. Although the *sertão* would later be inscribed with the promises of wealth and abundance, perhaps the abiding symbolic value of the *sertão* remains its capacity to express uncivilized, strange, dangerous, and even savage Otherness. As such, studying the cartographic record facilitates our understanding of Portugal's colonial expansion, exploration of Brazil's vast interior, and encounters with indigenous peoples. Nevertheless, the history and symbolic appropriation of the *sertão* as idealized Other suggest the scope of the difficulties that residents of the *sertão* continue to face today as they seek greater political representation and inclusion within Brazilian society.

[43]   Kalina Silva, p. 43.

A Poetry of Flesh and Bone:
Miguel de Unamuno and Miguel Torga

ROBERT PATRICK NEWCOMB

University of California, Davis

they, time overthrown,
Were dead yet flesh and bone.

(W. B. Yeats, 'The Double Vision of
Michael Robartes', 1919)

One might organize a comparative study of the poetry of Miguel de Unamuno (Spain, 1864–1936) and Miguel Torga (Portugal, 1907–1995) in a number of ways, beginning with the question of influence. While there is no evidence to suggest that Unamuno was aware of Torga, who began his literary career just eight years before the Spanish poet's death, Torga was quite familiar with Unamuno, and was amply influenced by him.[1] Indeed, the poet born Adolfo Correia da Rocha to peasant parents in rural Trás-os-Montes was exceptional within twentieth-century Portuguese letters for his degree of interest in Spanish literature and culture, and for the extent of his travels in Spain. Rocha adopted 'Miguel Torga' as his literary alias in 1934 in partial homage to Unamuno. He placed Unamuno on a shortlist of 'venerated' writers in a 1950 personal profile, alongside Cervantes — the other Miguel honoured in Torga's pseudonym.[2] Torga wrote reverentially of Unamuno on several occasions in his sixteen-volume, self-published *Diário* (1932–93), while in the poem 'Unamuno' he praised the Salamanca rector as a fellow devotee of the Iberian countryside, '[a] requestar na carne da paisagem | A alma que, zeloso, protegia' [Searching in the flesh of the land | For the soul it zealously guarded].[3] References in Torga's diary to Unamuno's *En torno al casticismo* (1902), *Vida de Don Quijote y Sancho* (1905), and *Del sentimiento trágico de la vida* (1913) demonstrate his familiarity with the Spanish writer's major exegetic works, as does his use in his poetry and prose of terms coined or popularized by Unamuno, such as 'intrahistoria' [intrahistory], 'mi señor Don Quijote' [my Lord Don Quixote], and of greatest significance for this article, 'el hombre de carne y hueso' [the man of flesh and bone].[4]

---

[1]   I describe Unamuno's influence on Torga more extensively in my article 'Iberian Anguish: Unamuno's Influence on Miguel Torga', *Luso-Brazilian Review*, 49.2 (2012), 188–206.
[2]   Clara Rocha, *Miguel Torga: fotobiografia* (Lisbon: Publicações Dom Quixote, 2000), p. 100.
[3]   Miguel Torga, *Poesia completa*, 2 vols (Lisbon: Publicações Dom Quixote, 2007), II, 288.
[4]   Miguel Torga, *Diário*, 16 vols (Coimbra: self-published, 1941–93), I, 49; IV, 179; VII, 202; IX, 45, 111, 138.

Portuguese Studies vol. 30 no. 1 (2014), 21–36
© Modern Humanities Research Association 2014

As I have discussed elsewhere,[5] Unamuno and Torga shared a number of literary and intellectual preoccupations. Chief among these were an abiding concern for Spanish–Portuguese relations and an interest in fostering integrated forms of Iberian identity. Both men were controversial voices in their home countries, earning reputations as literary outliers, and they remain polemical figures in their respective national literary canons. This is due in part, I believe, to their active embrace of literary models from Portugal (in Unamuno's case) and Spain (Torga), as well as their understanding of Spanish and Portuguese literature, culture, and identity as deeply and inextricably intertwined. Indeed, Unamuno and Torga were unique within twentieth-century Spanish and Portuguese letters for their degree of engagement with writers, landscapes, and ideas from across the Luso-Hispanic frontier. Unamuno made various visits to northern Portugal, publishing his impressions in the volume *Por tierras de Portugal y de España* (1911) and in various other texts.[6] Unamuno's private library featured nearly three hundred titles written by Portuguese authors or concerning Lusophone topics.[7] He was well versed in Portuguese literature, particularly nineteenth-century writers, whom he tirelessly promoted to his Spanish-speaking readers: Camilo Castelo Branco, Antero de Quental, and Oliveira Martins were among Unamuno's favourites. He praised Castelo Branco's *Amor de perdição* (1862), for instance, as 'la novela de pasión amorosa más intensa y más profunda que se haya escrito en la Península' [the most intense and profound novel of romantic passion that has been written on the Peninsula]. He described Quental as 'la más trágica figura de nuestra literatura ibérica' [the most tragic figure of our Iberian literature]. And he celebrated Oliveira Martins as the Peninsula's 'único historiador artista' [only artistic historian].[8] Further, Unamuno befriended and championed living Portuguese writers including Guerra Junqueiro, Eugénio de Castro, Teixeira de Pascoaes, and the young Vitorino Nemésio. And as I have contended elsewhere,[9] Unamuno viewed Iberia as a dialectical unity comprised of regions that were culturally, linguistically and tellurically distinct, but nonetheless interdependent. Indeed, he described Iberia on one occasion as a 'categoría histórica, por lo tanto espiritual, que ha hecho, en unidad, el alma de un territorio con sus contrastes y contradicciones interiores' [historical, and therefore spiritual category, that as a unity has formed the soul of a territory, in all of its contrasts and internal contradictions].

---

[5] See my 'Iberian Anguish'.
[6] See the articles written between 1912 and 1935, collected in the 'Letras portuguesas' section of volume II of Unamuno's *Obras completas*, as well as 'Prólogo a *Constanza* de Eugenio de Castro' (1913), 'Coimbra' (1914), 'Español-portugués' (1914), 'Portugal independiente' (1917), 'El sarcasmo ibérico de Eça de Queirós' (1917), 'Deber de España para con Portugal' (1917), and 'Lisboa y Toledo' (1935).
[7] *Epistolario portugués de Unamuno*, ed. by Ángel Marcos de Dios (Paris: Fundação Calouste Gulbenkian; Centro Cultural Português, 1978), pp. 363–74.
[8] Miguel de Unamuno, *Obras completas*, ed. by Manuel García Blanco (Madrid: Escelicer, 1966–71), I, 191; IV, 1329. All translations are my own.
[9] 'Portugal na visão unamuniana da Ibéria como unidade dialética', *Estudos Avançados*, 24.69 (2010), 61–78.

Within this unity, Unamuno believed that Portugal and Spain's manifold differences might, in Hegelian fashion, resolve themselves (*OC*, IV, 1081).

Torga, for his part, born in a region of Portugal bordered by Galicia and León, visited Spain countless times over his long life, recording his thoughts in his *Diário* and his multi-volume autobiographical novel *A criação do mundo* (1937–81). He also penned a series of *Poemas Ibéricos* (1965), which are among his best-known verses, and considered himself a 'português hispânico' [Hispanic Portuguese] and cultural Iberianist (*Diário*, XIV, 175).[10] Torga was a great admirer of Cervantes and of modern Spanish writers such as Antonio Machado and Federico García Lorca, whom he considered his 'vizinhos e contemporâneos' [neighbours and contemporaries] (*Diário*, XII, 197). Further, he praised the Spanish painters El Greco, Zurbarán, and Goya, and around 1930 began reading the 'Spanish agonists' Unamuno and Ángel Ganivet.[11] Moreover, Torga associated a series of laudable — albeit stereotyped — traits with what he, alongside numerous domestic and foreign commentators termed the 'génio espanhol' [Spanish genius] (*Diário*, VI, 29). In particular, Torga celebrated the prototypical Spaniard's apparently congenital obstinacy and heroic individualism, qualities Torga aligned with his own 'granitic' and 'monolithic' self-image (*Diário*, I, 119; XII, 76). On the whole, Spanish readers have received Torga's work favourably, with Torga's Spanish translator Eloísa Álvarez claiming that the writer's death in 1995 received greater attention in the Spanish press than in Portugal.[12]

Moving to their poetry, I would contend that Unamuno and Torga are best viewed as essentially *rural* poets, and of a particular sort. In accordance with Unamuno's affirmation that 'el campo es una metáfora' [the countryside is a metaphor], and Torga's notion (drawing, no doubt, on Amiel) that '[a] pais-agem é bem um estado de alma' [landscape is truly a matter of the soul] (Unamuno: *OC*, I, 494; Torga: *Diário*, IV, 150), Unamuno and Torga returned in their compositions to specific rugged landscapes — the Castilian *meseta* for

---

[10] Torga summarized his position on Iberia on 9 February 1983: '[U]m verdadeiro continente, pela singularidade da sua fisionomia física, rácica, idiomática, cultural, económica e política. Mais do que um conglomerado de regiões, um conjunto de nações [...] Nações unidas pela mesma fatalidade geográfica e por uma teia de cruzamentos históricos, mas tão vincadamente originais que as fronteiras de cada uma, mais do que no mapa, estão traçadas na alma de cada filho' [A true continent, for the singularity of its physical, racial, linguistic, cultural, economic, and political physiognomy [...] Nations united by the same fatality of geography and by a web of historical intersections, but so individually marked that the edges of each one are traced on the soul of each of its sons rather than on a map] (*Diário*, XIV, 36).
[11] Eduardo Novo Palacio, 'El sentimiento ibérico en la obra poética torguiana', in *Literatura portuguesa y literatura española: influencias y relaciones*, anejo no. XXXI de la *Revista Cuadernos de Filología*, Universitat de València, 1999, p. 315.
[12] Eloísa Álvarez, 'A imprensa espanhola perante a morte de Miguel Torga', in *Dar mundo ao coração: estudos sobre Miguel Torga*, ed. by Carlos Mendes de Sousa (Alfragide, Portugal: Texto Editores; Fundação Calouste Gulbenkian, 2009), pp. 39–50. For Torga's reception in Spain, see also José María Moreiro, *Eu, Miguel Torga*, trans. by Carlos Bento (Algés, Portugal: Difusão Editorial, 2001), p. 105. See also Álvarez quoted in João Céu e Silva, *Uma longa viagem com Miguel Torga* (Porto: Edições ASA, 2007), p. 282.

Unamuno and Trás-os-Montes for Torga. Further, they described and identified themselves with the natural and human features of these landscapes — what Unamuno termed their 'paisaje y paisanaje' [physical and human landscapes] (*OC*, I, 705). At the metatextual level, the two poets habitually utilize terms and motifs drawn in equal parts from the natural and corporeal worlds, including ground (*suelo/chão*), stone (*piedra/pedra*), skeleton (*esqueleto*), entrails (*entrañas/ entranhas*) — and as we shall see presently, flesh (*carne*) and bone (*hueso/osso*). In broad terms, we might describe the overlapping Unamunian and Torgian poetic approaches as strongly autobiographical,[13] generally rural, marked by religious imagery, and concerned with the struggles of living, breathing 'men of flesh and bone'.[14]

With so many points of contact between Unamuno and Torga, both exceptionally long-lived and prolific writers, perhaps the most feasible strategy for undertaking a comparative study of their poetry is to select a specific figure that runs through the work of both men. As indicated above, in this article I will look to the idea of 'flesh and bone' (*carne y hueso/carne e osso*) for this purpose. This phrase remits to the Old and New Testaments,[15] and as an appendage to the dualistic opposition between *cuerpo* and *alma* that has been noted as a historical feature of Spanish literature,[16] it features sporadically in earlier Iberian poets.[17] However, 'flesh and bone' appears with such frequency in Unamuno and Torga, and is so resonant in their work, that it can be considered a typifying feature of these two poets and evidence of the former's strong influence on the latter. In the following analysis, I will focus on three connotations of 'flesh and bone' to be observed in Unamuno and Torga: these are *filiation*, *concreteness*, and *mutual dependence*. I will argue that Unamuno and Torga's variegated usage of 'flesh and bone' works to centre their poetry on those individuals Unamuno famously termed at the opening of his study *Del sentimiento trágico de la vida* as 'hombres de carne y hueso' [men of flesh and bone], that is, substantive, living and breathing — in short, 'real' — men and

---

[13] On Torga's pervasive *euismo* ['I-ism'], which he shares with Unamuno, see António Freire, *Lendo Miguel Torga* (Porto: Edições Salesianas, 1990), p. 100.

[14] Chorão writes of Torga's 'indefectível fidelidade à nossa condição carnal' [indefatigable faithfulness to our carnal condition]. João Bigotte Chorão, 'Como é Torga?', *Revista Colóquio/Letras*, 98 (July 1987), 19–21 (p. 20).

[15] Porter writes: '[D]id not Scripture teach that man was created by the Father in His own image, and that God Himself became flesh and died upon the Cross? Incarnation was crucial to the Passion [...] And, as prefigured by Christ's death and resurrection, in the flesh man would finally rise again [...] Far from washing its hands, Christianity thus implicated itself utterly in the dilemmas and dramas of the flesh'. Roy Porter, *Flesh in the Age of Reason* (New York: W. W. Norton, 2004), p. 19.

[16] See Dinko Cvitanovic, 'De la "Disputa" medieval al "Pleito" calderoniano', in *La idea del cuerpo en las letras españolas*, ed. by Dinko Cvitanovic (Bahia Blanca, Argentina: Instituto de Humanidades, Universidad Nacional del Sur, 1973), pp. 11–45. See also Porter (pp. 28–43) on this dualism in the broader West.

[17] See examples of 'carne y hueso' in eclogues by Encina and Garcilaso and in Garcilaso's sonnet 'Un rato se levanta mi esperanza...'. Juan del Encina, *Obras completas I*, ed. by Ana María Rambaldo (Madrid: Espasa-Calpe, 1978), p. 204; Garcilaso de la Vega, *Obras*, ed. by T. Navarro Tomás (Madrid: Espasa-Calpe, 1958), pp. 70, 205.

women, as opposed to humanity considered in the abstract. Further, in tracing
these connotations of 'flesh and bone' back to the Bible,[18] I will speak to the
marked presence of biblical and more broadly religious imagery and language
in the work of the two poets, both of whom were raised in strongly Catholic
environments, and who maintained a conflicted, agonic attitude toward God.[19]
Notwithstanding Unamuno's influence on Torga, differences may be observed
between Unamuno and Torga's poetic references to 'flesh and bone'. As we shall
see, these differences are due to a significant degree to the distinction between
Unamuno's desperate faith in God, and Torga's agonized atheism.

Bone of my bones, and flesh of my flesh

And Adam said, This [is] now bone of my bones, and flesh of my flesh.[20]
(Genesis 2. 23)

Of the three connotations of 'flesh and bone' identified above, Unamuno and
Torga give the most limited treatment to *filiation*, by which I mean the use of
'flesh and bone' to suggest what in English we term 'blood' ties.[21] Nonetheless,
interesting observations can be made. In a section of his long poem *El Cristo de
Velázquez* (1920), a meditation on Velázquez's painting of the *Cristo crucificado*
(*c.* 1632), Unamuno transposes the biblical Adam and Eve onto the figure of
the crucified Christ, referring to Genesis 2. 23, in which Adam describes his
relationship to Eve by declaring her, 'bone of my bones, and flesh of my flesh'.
Unamuno's intention in this section of the poem (whose title, 'Pecho', indirectly
recalls the biblical account of God's creation of Eve from Adam's rib), and
more generally in *El Cristo de Velázquez*, seems to be to affirm the common
parentage and shared, corporeal humanity of modern men and women with
biblical figures, particularly Jesus Christ. Just as Adam describes Eve in Genesis
as 'bone of my bones', Unamuno describes humankind's filial relationship to
Christ:

> Recia fábrica
> dentro de este tu pecho, de costillas

[18]   On Torga's 'deep knowledge' of the Bible, see Isabel Vaz Ponce de Leão, *O essencial sobre Miguel
Torga* (Lisbon: Imprensa Nacional–Casa da Moeda, 2003), p. 4. For Torga's preference for the Old
Testament, see Teresa Rita Lopes, *Miguel Torga: ofícios a 'um Deus de Terra'* (Rio Tinto, Portugal:
Edições ASA, 1993), p. 36. For his specific affinity for the Book of Job, see Eduardo Lourenço, *O
desespero humanista de Miguel Torga e o das novas gerações* (Coimbra: Coimbra Editora, 1955), p. 47.
[19]   Unamuno's agonized faith is illustrated in *Del sentimiento trágico de la vida* and *La agonía
del cristianismo* (1931), among other texts. For agony and anguish in Torga, see Carlos Carranca,
Casticismo em Unamuno e Torga (Coimbra: MinervaCoimbra, 2012), p. 18; Helena Carvalhão Buescu,
'Da expressão à tensão: o fundamento agónico em Miguel Torga', in *Aqui, neste lugar e nesta hora: actas
do Primeiro Congresso Internacional sobre Miguel Torga* (Porto: Universidade Fernando Pessoa, 1994),
pp. 91–96; Ponce de Leão (pp. 71, 86–87).
[20]   All English-language biblical quotations are taken from the King James Version.
[21]   In English one speaks of 'blood' ties as opposed to ties of 'flesh and bone', and 'men of flesh and
blood' instead of 'men of flesh and bone' in reference to 'real' or substantive men. Unamuno explains
this difference in 'La personalidad de la voz' (1924) (*OC*, VII, 920).

viriles como aquellas de que hiñera
tu Padre a la mujer, porque eres, Cristo,
de nuestros huesos, hueso. (*OC*, VI, 474)

[Rough fabric,
within this your chest, of ribs
sturdy like those from which your Father
made woman, because you, Christ, are
bone of our bones.]

Perhaps recalling the biblical account of God's creation of Adam from dust and subsequent curse of him, in Genesis 3. 19 ('for dust thou [art], and unto dust shalt thou return'), Unamuno grants the phrase 'bone of my bones, and flesh of my flesh' a telluric dimension. He describes Christ's relationship to the Virgin Mary *qua* 'Mother Earth' as mediated through His body, that is, 'bones of the Earth's bones':

Tras este velo de tu carne anúnciase
la osamenta, la roca de tu cuerpo,
que es hueso de los huesos de la Tierra,
que es roca de la roca de tu Madre. (*OC*, VI, 475)

[Behind this veil of your flesh there lie
the bones, the rock of your body,
that is bone of the Earth's bones,
that is rock of your Mother's rock.]

Unamuno, gesturing toward the concrete humanity of the 'hombre concreto, el de carne y hueso' [concrete man, of flesh and bone] (*OC*, VII, 109) whom he defends in *Del sentimiento trágico de la vida* as the proper focus of metaphysical and religious inquiry, asserts in *El Cristo de Velázquez* that humankind's filial relationship to Jesus Christ (i.e. humankind as 'children of God') is defined in carnal or corporeal terms: our collective dependence on Christ for salvation is, for Unamuno, mediated through Christ's body, and is predicated on the bodily death of Christ as a living, breathing, *suffering* being.[22] Further, this relationship and the salvation it promises are imperilled by the possibility of our own bodily corruption, whether figurative (through sin), or literal (in sickness and death), a process of decay from which Christ, though He possessed 'real' flesh, was exempt.[23] Referring to the Last Judgment, Unamuno asks: '¿Vendrás, Señor, en

---

[22] Unamuno in his *Diario íntimo* insisted on Christ's carnal humanity: 'Humanos son hambre, sed, calor, hielo, pena, desgracia, persecuciones, sueño y fatiga. Todas estas son cosas que también Cristo padeció en sí, el cual era un verdadero hombre para nosotros y con nosotros' [Humans are hunger, thirst, heat, cold, pain, disgrace, persecution, dreams and fatigue. Christ, like us, suffered all of these things, and he was truly a man for us and like us] (*OC*, VIII, 812). Here and in *El Cristo de Velázquez* Unamuno may draw for inspiration on Lope's account of the Passion in his *Rimas sacras*, with its references to Christ's *entrañas* [entrails], *carne* [flesh], and *sangre* [blood]. Lope de Vega, *Poesías líricas II*, ed. by José F. Montesinos (Madrid: Espasa-Calpe, 1952), pp. 92–93. See also Porter (p. 36).
[23] Encina describes Christ's simultaneously carnal and divine nature as follows: '[E]s perfeto Dios hombre, | hombre de alma racional, | hombre de carne humanal, | es hombre y hombre su nombre' [God is perfect and a man | a man with a reasoning soul, | a man of human flesh, | He is a man and

carne y hueso al cabo | de los días mortales?' [Will you come, Lord, in flesh and bone at the end | of earthly days?], and 'el rocío | de tu sangre a esos huesos levantados | ¿los hará florecer en viva carne?' [the dew | of your blood, to these risen bones | will it bring them to flower in living flesh?] (*OC*, VI, 476).

Torga was an avowed non-believer, though a man who despite his atheism was persistently haunted by God and by questions of faith. Eduardo Lourenço proposed, accurately I think, that 'Torga não acredita, mas desejaria poder acreditar' [Torga does not believe, but he would like to be able to believe].[24] The former seminarian characterized himself in his *Diário* as 'um ateu a conviver com divindades desde a pia baptismal' [an atheist who has lived with the divine from the baptismal font'] (*Diário*, XI, 176).[25] Torga joins Unamuno in invoking the biblical phrase 'bone of my bones, and flesh of my flesh' in his poetry and repeatedly gestures toward bodily corruption as a signifier of humankind's irredeemably earthly and mortal (one might say fallen) condition. Although unlike Unamuno, whose lifelong struggle with belief was premised, as for Kierkegaard, on the ultimate necessity of God's existence, Torga understood humankind's existence on Earth as occurring in the absence of God. He makes this apparent in his 1942 poem 'Sangue', in which he describes a poet 'cá neste mundo, | Infeliz, | Só e senhor de si' [here in this world, | Disgraced, | Alone and left to himself], who is forced to take on an absent God's role as creator. Torga's creator-poet contemplates a real or imagined son whom he describes, as with God in relation to Christ, or Adam in relation to Eve, as '[c]arne da sua carne' [flesh of his flesh] (*Poesia completa*, I, 143). Further, God's absence seems to compel Torga toward descriptions of human flesh as *necessarily* rotting or corrupted, that is, as consigned to decay and death without the possibility of salvation. For instance, Torga's poem 'Cântico',[26] despite the hymn-like quality of its title, describes a:

> Mundo do mesmo barro
> De que somos feitos.
> Carne da nossa carne
> Apodrecida.
> Mundo que o tempo gasta e arrefece,
> Mas único jardim que se conhece
> Onde floresce a vida. (*Poesia completa*, II, 134)

His name is man] (p. 164). See also John Donne's sonnet 'Resurrection', for the incorruptibility of Christ's flesh: 'Flesh in that long sleep is not putrified'. Donne, *The Complete English Poems*, ed. by C. A. Patrides (London: Dent, 1985), p. 433.

[24] Lourenço, p. 35.

[25] For views that emphasize Torga's tendencies toward pantheism and folk Christianity, see Maria Fernanda Angius, 'O sentimento do sagrado na obra de um ateu', in *Aqui, neste lugar e nesta hora: actas do Primeiro Congresso Internacional sobre Miguel Torga* (Porto: Universidade Fernando Pessoa, 1994), pp. 35–45; Carlos Carranca, *Torga: o bicho religioso*, 2nd edn (Lisbon: Universitária Editora, 2000), pp. 20, 23; Lourenço, p. 47.

[26] Several of Torga's poems are *cânticos* [canticles]. In 'Cântico de Humanidade', he writes: 'Hinos aos deuses, não. | Os homens é que merecem' [Hymns to the gods, no. | It is men who deserve them] (*Poesia completa*, I, 321).

[World of the same clay
Of which we are made.
Flesh of our flesh
Rotted.
A world that time wears away and cools,
But the only garden I know of
Where life springs forth.]

With no possibility of eternal life — a state of affairs Unamuno would have found intolerable — Torga presents Earth as the sole arena of human existence and aspiration, the only context in which religious or metaphysical longing may occur. For us there is, as Torga starkly relates in 'Claro-Escuro', '[e]sta brutalidade, e nada mais' [this brutality, and nothing more] (*Poesia completa*, II, 123), though, importantly, this does not negate our desire for transcendence. As Torga stated in a public address given on his eightieth birthday, and utilizing a paradoxically religious language: 'Acredito piamente que é neste pobre planeta que tudo se processa e vale ou não vale a pena. Que é aqui que nos cumprimos ou negamos, que nos transcendemos ou não, dando à vida a dignidade que ela merece, por ser o supremo bem' [I devoutly believe that it is on this poor planet where everything occurs and is or it not worth the cost. That it is here where we fulfil or deny ourselves, where we transcend ourselves or do not, where we give life the dignity it deserves, as the supreme good] (*Diário*, XV, 59–60). Returning to 'Cântico', we see that Torga suggestively alters 'flesh of my flesh' to allow for the idea of the human collectivity. He refers to 'carne da *nossa* carne' [flesh of our flesh], and modifies the term *carne* with the adjective *apodrecida* [rotted], as if to imply that our filiation with one another and shared earthly condition do not exempt us from bodily decay and death. In a diary entry dated 15 December 1942, Torga bemoans how 'esta carne apodrece' [this flesh rots], and asks rhetorically, 'quem é que se pode libertar dos pés que o ligam ao chão? Somos de terra, amigos' [Who can cut himself loose from the feet that tie him to the ground? Friends, we are of the earth] (*Diário*, II, 94, 96). Indeed, for Torga interpersonal solidarity is intimately tied to, even predicated on, the shared 'corruption' of our flesh, that is, our common mortality, a condition we may describe using Torga's suggestive image of a 'fraternidade dos ossos' [fraternity of bones] (*Diário*, II, 12). In this respect, Torga again resembles Unamuno, who though desperate to believe in an afterlife, viewed bodily death as *the* great problem of human existence.[27]

[27] See from Unamuno's *Diario íntimo*: 'Es una cosa que me extraña cómo puede haber personas a quienes no conmueva y agite y desazone la idea del aniquilamiento, que crean fríamente en él y vivan, o que vivan sin pensar que han de morir. ¿Serán de otra madera que yo?' [It puzzles me how there can be people whom death does not move, nor trouble, nor disturb, nor upset, who coldly accept death and go on living, or who live without thinking that one day they will die. Are they made from different stuff than I am?] (*OC*, VIII, 826). For Torga on death, see his diary entry for 8 June 1953: 'Seres irremediàvelmente mortais, é nesta vida apenas que terão de desatar o nó dos mistérios, e nela também serão obrigados ao heroísmo de amar o absoluto no relativo' [Irremediably mortal beings, humans have only this lifetime to untie the knot of life's mysteries, and to be called to heroically love the absolute from the standpoint of relativity] (*Diário*, VII, 12). See also for 4 February 1986: 'Beber estoicamente até

Skin and flesh, bones and sinews

Thou hast clothed me with skin and flesh,
and hast fenced me with bones and sinews. (Job 10. 11)

Unamuno and Torga give more extensive treatment to *concreteness* as a connotation of 'flesh and bone', utilizing this phrase to insist on the substantive humanity of the men and women the poets describe elsewhere as joined in shared suffering. Moving beyond the famous example from his *Del sentimiento trágico de la vida* of the 'hombre de carne y hueso', that is, 'el que nace, sufre y muere — sobre todo muere — , el que come, y bebe, y juega, y duerme, y piensa, y quiere: el hombre que se ve y a quien se oye, el hermano, el verdadero hermano' [the man of flesh and bone, he who is born, who suffers and dies — above all dies — , he who eats, and drinks, and plays, and sleeps, and thinks, and wants: the man whom we see and hear, our brother, our true brother] (*OC*, VII, 109), Unamuno invokes 'flesh and bone' with reference to real, substantive men and women on several other occasions (*OC*, VII, 109). For instance, in a section of *El Cristo de Velázquez* entitled 'Eucaristía', Unamuno gestures toward Christ's corporeality as evidence for His 'concrete humanity',[28] which he argues is, in turn, the key to humankind's 'carnal hunger' for Christ as the guarantor of our salvation. Invoking the oft-repeated John 1. 14 ('And the Word was made flesh, and dwelt among us') and inserting himself into the theological debate on Christ's flesh (*sarx*) in John,[29] Unamuno declares: '¡Carne de Dios, Verbo encarnado, encarna | nuestra divina hambre carnal de Ti!' [Flesh of God, Word made flesh, embody | our divine carnal hunger for You!] (*OC*, VI, 444). Earlier in *El Cristo de Velázquez*, in a section titled 'Ecce Homo', Unamuno draws on the tradition of the suffering Christ in describing 'el Hombre-Dios, Hijo del hombre' [the Man-God, Son of man], and affirms the direct causal relationship between the flagellation of Christ's flesh (here a synecdoche for Christ himself) and the possibility of our salvation:

> sólo Tú, la carne que padece,
> la carne de dolor que se desangra,
> a las entrañas nos la diste en pábulo,
> pan de inmortalidad a los mortales. (*OC*, VI, 422)
>
> [only You, the suffering flesh,
> the pained flesh that bleeds,

à última gota o cálice de amargura da vida. É o meu ponto de honra' [To stoically drink to the last drop from the chalice of life's bitterness: this is my point of honour] (*OC*, XIV, 182).
[28] Martinus C. De Boer, 'The Death of Jesus Christ and His Coming in the Flesh (1 John 4:2)', *Novum Testamentum*, Vol. 33, Fasc. 4 (Oct. 1991), p. 326.
[29] For an overview of the debate, see De Boer and Thompson. Unamuno's position approximates the 'sarctic' interpretation, which emphasizes the centrality of Christ's human incarnation for human salvation. Marianne Meye Thompson, *The Humanity of Jesus in the Fourth Gospel* (Philadelphia, PA: Fortress, 1988), pp. 33–52; Henry Staten, 'How the Spirit (Almost) Became Flesh: Gospel of John', *Representations*, 41 (Winter 1993), 34–57 (p. 35).

from your entrails you gave as fuel,
bread of immortality to us, mortal men.]

Like Unamuno, Torga repeatedly utilizes the figure of 'flesh and bone',
and more specifically, Unamuno's 'man of flesh and bone', to suggest the
idea of a concrete, substantive — in short 'real' — humanity. Further, Torga
grants the struggles of his *homens de carne e osso* a metaphysical if not overtly
religious dimension, and draws on biblical stories and motifs in doing so.
Unlike Unamuno, though, Torga's biblically inspired descriptions present God
as alternately absent or oppressive, describe death without the possibility of
salvation as inevitable, and declare the poet's personal lack of faith. Torga's
collection *O outro livro de Job* (1936), which contains several poems dealing with
scripture and with questions of belief, includes three 'lamentations', in which the
poet bemoans the human condition while referring to specific biblical episodes.
In the 'Primeira Lamentação', which, in addition to making titular reference to
the Book of Lamentations, refers to Adam, St Peter and the frequently employed
biblical metaphor of sheep gone astray, Torga distinguishes between humankind
at large (*Homem*) and individuals such as himself (*homens*). He thereby makes
explicit the idea that his individual struggles are part of a larger human story,
that he 'eterniz[a] | O mesmo Homem de sempre' [eternalizes | The same Man
as always], and that our collective suffering is due to our lot as mortal men and
women limited to one life on Earth:

> Tudo
> Por causa da minha Fé
> Na minha sabedoria
> De andar em pé!...
>
> Tudo
> Por eu ser um pobre vivo
> A eternizar
> O mesmo Homem de sempre
> Com raízes
> Que ninguém pode arrancar...
>
> O Homem de carne e osso
> Que tu não mudas e eu não mudo!
>   (*Poesia completa*, I, 54)[30]
>
> [Everything
> Because of my Faith
> In my ability
> To keep walking!...
>
> Everything

---

[30]   For more 'men of flesh and bone' in Torga, see 'Eco' ('Ah, terra transmontana | Que não tens um
cantor à tua altura! | [...] De carne e osso') [Oh, land of Trás-os-Montes | Without a man of your stature
| [...] of flesh and bone, to sing of you!] (*Poesia completa*, II, 341). See also Torga, *Diário*, VII, 103; XI,
104.

Because I am a poor mortal
Eternalizing
The same Man as always
With roots
No one can pull up...

The Man of flesh and bone
That neither you nor I can change!]

In his 'Segunda Lamentação', Torga adopts the voice of Adam expelled from Eden, questioning his state as a man condemned to mortality and destined to become an 'esqueleto descarnado | Que está no chão desenhado | A apodrecer' [skeleton without flesh | On the ground destined | To rot] (*Poesia completa*, I, 57).

In his 1943 collection *Lamentação*, Torga again takes up the distinction between abstract humanity and living, breathing men and women, interrogating one 'Senhor Homem', an authoritarian figure who takes on the guise of biblical figures, and of God himself. Torga blames 'Senhor Homem' for the suffering of those Unamuno would term *hombres de carne y hueso*. Writing against the backdrop of the Second World War, Torga condemns 'Senhor Homem' for the corruption of the modern world: 'Quando no plaino lírico do tempo | te vejo na legítima pureza; | [...] | chego a pensar que a terra apodreceu' [With time having lyrically planed you down | I see you in your true, pure state; [...] I come to think that the Earth has rotted]. And returning to the figure of 'flesh and bone', he describes the horror of life under 'Senhor Homem', as 'um luto em carne e osso' [mourning in flesh and bone] (*Poesia completa*, I, 133). In Nietzschean fashion, Torga offers that life will be more bearable after his 'death', which we might interpret as tantamount to a mass abandonment of an oppressive God in favour of a collective, secular rededication to bonds of interpersonal solidarity.

Significantly, Torga follows Unamuno in implying that the distinction between abstract humanity (*Homem, Senhor Homem*) and concrete men and women (*homens, homens de carne e osso*) is typological rather than absolute. Just as we can — and according to Unamuno and Torga, should — understand ourselves as living, breathing men and women, so may we identify ourselves abstractly, as part of the category of *humanitas*. For both writers, the tendency toward abstraction is problematic. For Unamuno it risks obscuring 'men of flesh and bone' as the proper focus of philosophical and religious inquiry. For Torga, rather, it opens the door to oppression of others or the self — possibly at the hands of a despotic God or Church:

Tirano do irmão que em ti vivia,
e déspota dos próprios pensamentos,
eras tu aquele réu que se cumpria
conforme os seus humanos mandamentos!
(*Poesia completa*, I, 132)

[A tyrant to the brother who lived within you,
and a despot to your own thoughts,

It was you, you are that criminal that came to be
through his human commandments!]

Or as Torga observed in a diary entry dated 24 October 1960: 'Quando o homem sublima as coisas, nascem os deuses pagãos; quando sublima o semelhante, nasce Cristo; quando se sublima a si próprio, nasce o tirano' [When man sublimates things, pagan gods are born; when he sublimates his neighbour, Christ is born; when he sublimates himself, tyrants are born] (*Diário*, IX, 45).

Penas do Purgatório (1954) presents us with yet another Torga collection whose title has a religious resonance. The volume opens with the poet's declaration of unbelief: 'Não tenho deuses. Vivo | Desamparado. | Sonhei deuses outrora, | Mas acordei' [I have no gods. I live | Uncared for. | I dreamt of gods at one time, | But I woke up] (*Poesia completa*, II, 29). Further, the volume includes a poem, 'Drama', which reads as a distillation of the tragic condition of the Unamunian 'man of flesh and bone', which, as I have argued, Torga adapts to a fundamentally atheistic worldview — though one nonetheless steeped in religious traditions and language.[31] Indeed, 'Drama' contains a reference to transfiguration — one of several in Torga's work — though as the poet implies, his earthly, 'animal' condition as 'all flesh and bone'[32] precludes the possibility of such transfiguration:

> Todo de carne e osso,
> Como posso
> Transfigurar-me?
> A vara de condão que me levanta
> Ergue o peso dum homem.
> Sou maciço, animal. (*Poesia completa*, II, 37)

> [All flesh and bone,
> How can I
> Be transfigured?
> The sorcerer's wand that lifts me up
> Has the weight of a man.
> I am solid, an animal.]

Of his flesh, and of his bones

For we are members of his body, of his flesh, and of his bones.
(Ephesians 5. 30)

Finally, we arrive at the image of the integrated, living body, composed of flesh and bones. I argue that in Unamuno and Torga alike this body is suggestive of the notion of *mutual dependence*, whether understood in terms of internal

---

[31]   See also Lourenço (p. 38), who cites 'Drama' as evidence of Torga's Unamunian preoccupation with the problem of human immortality.
[32]   Thompson (p. 44) notes the common Old Testament usage of the phrase 'all flesh' to indicate an individual's concrete humanity. Torga's '[t]odo de carne e osso' [all flesh and bone] recalls this usage.

bodily functions, interpersonal or communal relationships, or relations *between* landscapes or regions *within* a broader unity, such as Iberia. Just as Unamuno presents Christ's body in *El Cristo de Velázquez* as an integrated system, writing in a section entitled 'Osamenta', '[t]ras este velo de tu carne anúnciase | la osamenta, la roca de tu cuerpo' [behind the veil of your flesh there lie | the bones, the rock of your body] (*OC*, VI, 475), he presents Spain — and more broadly, Iberia — in corporeal terms. For Unamuno, this Peninsular body is composed metaphorically of both 'flesh' and 'bone', which must work together to ensure the health of the whole, and for which, as with the analogy between Christ's body and 'the communal Body' of believers, 'the relationship between parts is as important as that between parts and whole. Only when each part becomes a member of each other part', that is, when flesh and bone are inextricably bonded together, 'is the communal Body whole'.[33] In an untitled poem from his *Cancionero* (1928–36), Unamuno writes of the Peninsula's 'arms' 'desparram[ando] y acarici[ando] | sobre hueso, carne parda, | que sangre y sudor hostigan' [spilling and caressing | over bone, brown flesh | whipped by blood and sweat] (*OC*, VI, 1097). And in the roughly contemporaneous essay, 'País, paisaje, y paisanaje' (1933), he describes Spain as a hand, with Iberia's five major rivers (four of which flow through Portugal, incidentally) its 'cinco dedos líquidos' [five liquid fingers] (*OC*, I, 705).

Writing against the backdrop of Spain's protracted imperial decline, which reached its culmination in the *desastre* of 1898, as well as significant regionalist agitation at the turn of the twentieth century, Unamuno offers a vision of Spain (and by extension, Iberia) as a dialectical unity. For Unamuno, then, regional differences and internal contradictions within Iberia need not be glossed over, but rather may be paradoxically brought into relief, so as to be resolved into a higher unity. This differentiated yet internally integrated view of Iberia lends itself to bodily metaphors, and helps explain Unamuno's tendency to deploy his favoured images of *carne* and *hueso* in counterbalancing certain 'bony' Iberian landscapes such as Castile, which he termed 'una tierra en esqueleto' [a skeletal land], and languages like Castilian, which he considered 'rígida y ósea' [rigid and bony], against 'fleshier' regions such as Galicia and northern Portugal, which he described as possessing 'un paisaje carnal' [a carnal landscape], and tongues like Portuguese and Galician, characterized by what Unamuno considered the untranslatable Galaico-Portuguese quality of '*meiguice*' (*OC*, I, 227–28, 383; IV, 332; VII, 557; original italic). For Unamuno, the Iberian 'body' requires flesh and bone, rivers and mountains, *meseta* and meadow to function. Similarly, the Galaico-Portuguese and Castilian languages and literary traditions, in Unamuno's view, will necessarily benefit from exchange and eventual integration.[34] This would explain why in his writings on Iberian identity

---

[33] Michael Bryson, 'Dismemberment and Community: Sacrifice and the Communal Body in the Hebrew Scriptures', *Religion & Literature*, 35.1 (Spring 2003), 1–21 (pp. 1–2).
[34] See the articles 'Español-portugués' (1914) and 'Hispanidad' (1927) (*OC*, IV, 526–29, 1081–84).

and geography, Unamuno consistently presents *carne* and *hueso* as mutually dependent. Indeed, Unamuno describes the metaphorical condition of being 'without flesh' or 'without bones' in terms of a potentially fatal lack. Referring to language, in a 1929 poem Unamuno plays on the double meaning in Spanish of *lengua* (tongue, language) in writing: 'Lengua, lengua, no lenguaje; | lengua que es carne sin hueso; | vendrá la letra, visaje, | calavera para el seso' [A tongue, a tongue, not a language; | a tongue that is flesh without bone; | the letter will arrive, a visual sign | a skull to hold the brain] (*OC*, VI, 1264). And in a letter to the writer Joan Maragall dated 19 December 1907, Unamuno described an embattled Portugal cut off from the rest of Iberia: '[E]se pobre país está perdido; [...] Se desprendió del hueso y ahora en carne pura, y en carne floja aunque sonrosada, empieza a marchitarse' [This poor country is lost; [...] It has fallen off the bone and now, all flesh, and now with loose but pink flesh, it begins to wither].[35] It is easy to understand Unamuno's poetic logic: a body composed of 'all flesh' or 'all bones' would necessarily die, whether we think in terms of real human bodies or broader geographic, cultural, and linguistic systems.[36]

Like Unamuno, Torga often described landscapes,[37] and specifically Iberian landscapes, in corporeal terms. This is the case in Torga's *Poemas Ibéricos* (1965), a series of poetic meditations on Iberian history and identity, with its references to 'o corpo da Ibéria' [the body of Iberia] and the 'humana terra de Castela' [human land of Castile] (*Poesia completa*, II, 247, 278). Also like Unamuno, Torga describes Peninsular landscapes as bodies metaphorically composed of flesh and bones that must work together to ensure the health of the whole. In a diary entry dated 7 December 1949 Torga wrote of his ongoing exegetic project to locate the essence of Portugal, using the image of a 'radiografia profunda, que revele a solidez do esqueleto sobre o qual todo o corpo se mantém' [powerful X-ray, capable of revealing the solidness of the skeleton that supports the entire body] (*Diário*, V, 61). In other words, Torga's inquiry was aimed at assessing the health of the national body by locating and inspecting its skeletal core (its *intrahistoria*, for Unamuno), which without scrutiny would remain hidden beneath the flesh. Further, Torga remarked decades later, in an entry dated 3 July 1975, of his *pátria* as the 'carne colectiva a que pertenço' [collective flesh to which I belong] (*Diário*, XII, 116). I find it significant that, in this entry, it is unclear whether Torga is referring to Portugal or Iberia at large. Indeed, he explained in a 1944 preface to the Spanish edition of his short story collection *Bichos* (1940): 'A minha pátria cívica acaba em Barca de Alva' [My civic homeland ends at Barca de Alva], that is, on the Portuguese frontier,

[35] Miguel de Unamuno & Juan Maragall, *Epistolario entre Miguel de Unamuno y Juan Maragall y escritos complementarios* (Barcelona: Edimar, 1951), p. 78.
[36] See from an unnamed poem by Unamuno: 'Tierra descarnada, parda | hueso ya tu corazón; | tierra descarnada, aguarda | tu final resurrección' [Land without flesh, brown | your heart turned to bone; | Land without flesh, you await | your final resurrection] (*OC*, VI, 1219).
[37] See, for instance, his references to the 'corpo' [body] of a mountain in 'Divindade', to the 'corpo violado da paisagem' [violated body of the land] in 'Incursão', and to the 'carne da paisagem' [flesh of the land] in 'Unamuno' (*Poesia completa*, I, 196; II, 153, 288).

'mas a minha pátria telúrica só finda nos Pireneus [...] Sou, pela graça da vida, peninsular' [but my telluric country only ends at the Pyrenees [...] I am, by the grace of life, Peninsular] (*Diário*, III, 47).

At certain moments in his poetry Torga invests this corporeal language of mutual dependence with telluric resonances and an overtly critical dimension, describing and denouncing a Portuguese national body, ailing under the stultifying influence of dictatorship, in terms of non-complementarity or imbalances of flesh and bone. This is the case in 'Litania' (1947), which we may add to the list of Torga's religiously inspired titles:

> S. Salvador do Mundo... de granito:
> Que salvaste, afinal?
> Ossos e ossos deste velho mito
> Que, sem terra, se chama Portugal.
>
> Nós nas giestas pedem-te, devotos,
> Carne de alcova, húmus de semente.
> E são fragas que dás, beijos remotos
> Num corpo que no céu há-de ser quente.
>
> S. Salvador do Mundo... português:
> Temos rezado tanto,
> E dás-nos este monte, esta aridez
> Feita pela erosão do nosso pranto!
>
> (Poesia completa, I, 338)

> [S. Salvador do Mundo... made of granite
> What, in the end, have you saved?
> Bone upon bone of this old myth
> That, landless, is called Portugal.
>
> Nodes in the brooms' stems ask you, devoutly,
> For the flesh of shelter, the humus of seeds,
> And you give us rocky hilltops, distant kisses
> On this body which will light itself up in the skies.
>
> S. Salvador do Mundo... of Portugal
> We have prayed and prayed,
> And you give us this mountain,
> Made barren by the erosion of our tears!]

Here, in a fashion similar to Unamuno, Torga links the motifs of bone and arid stone, of flesh and fertile earth, utilizing these linked motifs to critique Portuguese nationalism and popular religiosity, and unlike Unamuno, the impulse toward faith in a personal God.[38] Portugal's civil and religious institutions are represented by the mountain and chapel complex of São Salvador do Mundo, located in the interior of the Douro valley. The poet accuses 'São Salvador do Mundo' of saving nothing except the 'bones' or 'stones' of a failed

---

[38] As Torga notes in a 2 July 1966 diary entry: 'Os deuses são realmente respostas transitórias às nossas perguntas eternas' [Gods really are transitory answers to our eternal questions] (*Diário*, X, 94).

Portuguese national 'myth', while the people, consigned to an infertile land symbolized by the mountain, beg in vain for more 'flesh', that is, productive land and better living conditions.

* * * * *

While the figure of 'flesh and bone' may appear frequently in Western poetry,[39] and with particular frequency in Peninsular verse, images of flesh and bone are nonetheless especially resonant in the work of Miguel de Unamuno and Miguel Torga. Indeed, I have argued in this article that by attending to the connotations of 'flesh and bone' that manifest themselves in their poetry we may uncover a set of poetic values shared by these two writers, who despite Unamuno's significant degree of influence on Torga, are frequently viewed as literary outliers, if not writers who are frankly *sui generis*. At the centre of Unamuno and Torga's overlapping poetic approaches is the affirmation that the poet should, above all, attend to the struggles of the 'man of flesh and bone', who, lest we consign him to the status of rural, folkloric 'other', is, as Unamuno reminds us in *Del sentimiento trágico de la vida*, 'yo, tú, lector mío: aquel otro de más allá, cuantos pisamos sobre la tierra' [you, me, dear reader: that other man from over there, all who walk the Earth] (*OC*, VII, 109).

[39]   In addition to the Yeats poem quoted in this paper's epigraph, other examples of 'flesh and bone' in English-language poetry include Donne's 'A Valediction of my name, in the window' ('The rafters of my body, bone | Being still with you, the Muscle, Sinew, and Veine, | Which this house, will come againe') (p. 71), Milton's *Paradise Lost*, Book VIII ('Bone of my bone, flesh of my flesh, myself | Before me; woman is her name, of man | Extracted'), and several from Dylan Thomas, including 'Light Breaks Where No Sun Shines' ('The things of light | File through the flesh where no flesh decks the bones'), 'Ears in the Turrets Hear' ('Beyond this island bound | By a thin sea of flesh | and a bone coast'), and 'Find Meat on Bones' ('Rebel against the flesh and bone, | The word of the blood, the wily skin, | And the maggot no man can slay'). John Milton, *Paradise Lost*, ed. by David Scott Kastan (Indianapolis, IN: Hackett, 2005), p. 254; Dylan Thomas, *Collected Poems* (New York: New Directions, 1971), pp. 29, 67, 74.

The Mariquinhas Cycle:
An Ongoing Saga of Prostitution, Changing Values in Lisbon and Spleen for an Undefined Past

MICHAEL COLVIN

Marymount Manhattan College, NY

Since the mid-nineteenth century, prostitutes and ruffians have been the protagonists of Fado songs that take place in Lisbon's working-class neighbourhood of the Mouraria; and their sordid acts combined with a seemingly contrasting piety — born of their marginal, untouchable social status — has made them folkloric heroes: triumphant underdogs in an undemocratic Portugal.[1] Legendary figures such as Maria Severa, Rosa Maria and Cesária, and mythic personages like Chico do Cachené, Timpanas and tia Macheta are incarnations of an autonomous nineteenth-century Lisbon where caste seems to break down when aristocrats mingle with the *fadista* class of the Mouraria.[2] And in the twentieth century, these figures represent a Lisbon of another generation: memories archived in popular culture. Their persistence in the cast of characters in the theatre of the Fado is testament to the popular will to rescue the undocumented chronicle of Lisbon's underbelly as a means to subvert the state's erasure of an ignoble history.

But as the Estado Novo demolishes the western half of the Mouraria in its mid-twentieth-century public works projects, designed to bring progress and cleanliness to the 'cidade "abandonada e suja"' [dirty, abandoned city], the working-class setting of the vagrants' exploits also assumes top billing in the Fado's cast of characters.[3] As a result, Fado ballads whose setting is

[1] Thanks to Nuno Miguel Carvalho dos Santos whose questions about the relationship between 'Vou Dar de Beber à Dor' and 'Vou Dar de Beber à Alegria' compelled me to write this article.
[2] João Pinto de Carvalho, *História do fado* [1903] (Lisbon: Dom Quixote, 1992), gives brief biographies of Lisbon *fadistas*, Maria Severa Onofriana (1820–1846), Rosa Maria (early nineteenth century), and Cesária (A Mulher de Alcântara, late nineteenth century). *Fadista* Fernando Farinha (1928–1988) created the character of O Chico do Cachené in his eponymous Fado (1948); Timpanas and tia Macheta are characters in Júlio Dantas, *A Severa* [1901] (Porto: Porto Editora, 1973) and Júlio Dantas and André Brun, *A Severa* [1909] (Andre Brun, *A Severa: ópera cómica em três actos* (Porto: n.pub., 1912)).
[3] José-Augusto França, *Lisboa: urbanismo e arquitectura* (Lisbon: Instituto de Cultura e Língua Portuguesa, 1980), p. 98. (All translations from Portuguese are mine, unless otherwise stated). For more on twentieth-century urban planning in Lisbon, see Francisco Keil Amaral, *Lisboa, uma cidade em transformação* (Lisbon: Europa-América, 1969) and Marina Tavares Dias, *Lisboa desaparecida*, 9 vols (Lisbon: Quimera, 2007). For more on the Fado's reaction to the Estado Novo and the

Portuguese Studies vol. 30 no. 1 (2014), 37–46
© Modern Humanities Research Association 2014

an undefined but impoverished Lisbon are reset specifically in the Mouraria in sequels and homages that cannibalize the original verses. In Fernando Farinha's tribute to 'O Chico do Cachené', a wooden doll that decorated the shelves of the Adega Machado Fado house in the Bairro Alto, it is reanimated as a resident of the Mouraria in 'Ai Chico, Chico do Cachené', 'O Leilão', 'O Casino da Mariquinhas' and 'Já Sabem da Mariquinhas'.[4] In Julio Dantas's novel *A Severa* (1901), the character of Severa's real-life mother, the Mouraria prostitute Ana Gertrudes (alias Barbuda), is composed of biographical references to the nineteenth-century *fadista*, Cesária, a Mulher de Alcântara. The latter also appears, incongruously, as the protagonist of the operetta *Mouraria* (1926), by Lino Ferreira, Silva Tavares and Lopo Lauer.[5] Alfama brothel owner, Rosa Maria, becomes a condensed figure of herself and Mouraria streetwalker, Rosa Maria, in 'Há Festa na Mouraria', 'Fado Falado', 'O Zé Manel viu a Rosa Maria', 'O Leilão', 'Já Sabem da Mariquinhas', 'Chico Faia' and 'Fui ao Baile'.[6] The *cafés*

Câmara Municipal de Lisboa's twentieth-century urbanization projects, see Michael Colvin, *The Reconstruction of Lisbon: Severa's Legacy and the Fado's Rewriting of Urban History* (Lewisburg, PA: Bucknell University Press, 2008).

[4] Daniel Gouveia, *Biografias do fado: Fernando Farinha* (Lisbon: EMI, 1998), pp. 7–8, and Eduardo Sucena, *Lisboa, o fado e os fadistas* (Lisbon: Vega, 2002), pp. 127–29, explain that the Fado, 'O Chico do Cachené', started as a joke at the Adega Machado in 1941 when an audience member suggested that the house *fadistas* stage a musical trial about Tomás de Melo's well-dressed wooden doll, Chico, accused of 'viver à margem de bom senso' [living on the edge good sense] (Sucena, p. 127). According to Gouveia, Linhares Barbosa offered to write the music, and Fernando Farinha wrote the verses to 'O Chico do Cachené', in which the doll defends himself by telling the story of his good upbringing and his ill fate. In 1951, the *fadistas* at Café Luso in the Bairro Alto repeated the performance (pp. 7–8). According to Sucena, the improvisation took place on 25 May 1948 at the Café Luso where Linhares Barbosa played the role of the judge who declared Chico's innocence for 'se ter provado que era bom rapaz e... trabalhador' [having proven himself to be a good, hard-working kid] (p. 127).

[5] Sucena remarks (p. 40): 'embora soasse a falso o facto de se ter transplantado para a Mouraria (um bairro a que nada a ligava) a mulher de Alcântara, o certo é que, graças à história, à boa música e ao brilhante desempenho da actriz Adelina Fernandes, que no papel da protagonista (também desempenhado por Rafaela Haro) cantou o "Fado da Cesária", a operetta alcançou assinalado êxito' [even though it rang hollow that the *fadista* from Alcântara be transplanted to the Mouraria (a neighbourhood with which she had no connection), what is certain is that, thanks to history, great music, and the brilliant performance by Adelina Fernandes who, in the role of the protagonist (also played by Rafaela Haro), sang the 'Fado da Cesária', the operetta was a hit]. Rui Vieira Nery, *Para uma história do fado* (Lisbon: Público, 2004), p. 215, reflects: 'O Fado surge no seio da Revista sobretudo em quadros que procuram representar estereótipos da mitologia fadista, pondo em cena ora personagens-tipo como o faia, o marujo, a varina, a Severa, a Cesária, etc., ora figuras simbólicas representando a cidade de Lisboa ou qualquer dos seus bairros históricos' [The Fado takes centre stage in the *revista* [musical comedies], particularly in skits that attempt to represent stereotypes of the *fadista* mythology, sometimes focusing on stock characters like the *faia* [a stereotypical male member of the *fadista* class], the old salt, the fishwife, Severa, Cesária, etc., other times, symbolic figures representing the city of Lisbon or any of her historic neighbourhoods]; he also comments, 'o Fado evoca agora a Cesária, a Júlia Florista, a Rosa Maria e todas as grandes figuras míticas da sua era pioneira' [now the Fado evokes Severa, Cesária, Júlia Florista, Rosa Maria and all of the great mythic figures of its pioneering era] (p. 193).

[6] Colvin, *The Reconstruction of Lisbon* and 'Gabriel de Oliveira's "Há Festa na Mouraria" and the *Fado Novo*'s Criticism of the Estado Novo's Demolition of the Baixa Mouraria', *Portuguese Studies*, 20 (2004), 134–51, 'Há Festa na Mouraria', Gabriel de Oliveira / Alfredo Marceneiro; 'Há Festa na Mouraria', António Amargo / Alfredo Marceneiro; 'Fado Falado', Aníbal Nazaré / Nelson de Barros; 'O Zé Manel viu a Rosa Maria', M. Paião / A. Damas; 'O Leilão', Linhares Barbosa / Fado Corrido; 'Já Sabem da Mariquinhas', Carlos Conde / Fado Mouraria; 'Chico Faia', José Marques / Manuel Oliveira Santos; 'Fui ao Baile', Amadeu do Vale / Fernando de Carvalho.

de camareiras (a euphemism that translates as 'chambermaids' cafes'), early twentieth-century bars that doubled as points of assignation on the central streets off the Avenida da Liberdade, are recontextualized in the Mouraria in 'O Café de Camareiras', 'A Lucinda Camareira' and 'Encontrei a Marcelina'.[7] And Alfredo Marceneiro's 'A Casa da Mariquinhas' generates eleven songs about the apocryphal whorehouse whose original setting is never determined; of the twelve songs in the cycle, six are set in the Mouraria.

In 1930, Barreiro resident, Alfredo Duarte, better known as 'O Marceneiro' [the cabinet maker] because of his profession as a carpenter, first performed 'A Casa da Mariquinhas', Silva Tavares's ballad that describes the fictional whorehouse in Lisbon: 'É numa rua bizarra | A casa da Mariquinhas | Tem na sala uma guitarra | Janelas com tabuinhas' [Mariquinhas's house | Is located on a formidable street | There's a guitar in the parlour | And windows with shutters].[8] Marceneiro's original Fado is a narrative inventory of the bordello's interior decoration, the daily habits of the prostitutes who live and work there, and the reactions of the nosy neighbours who complain about the brothel's noisy parties. However, by the time Silva Tavares had penned the song's lyrics the legal Lisbon brothel had become clandestine and was on its way toward extinction. 'A Casa da Mariquinhas' is a nostalgic elegy to a codified Lisbon institution that was forced underground in a period of economic austerity and a politics of progress, deeply rooted in obedience to the regime and its overweening order.

But the Portuguese government already had sought to force the urban profession underground; thus, the Estado Novo's efforts to whitewash Lisbon were informed by a legislative tradition. Nearly a hundred years before the appearance of Marceneiro's Fado, the Liberal regime — following D. Pedro VI's amendment to the 1826 Constitution that had decreed a city-wide ban on prostitution — had tried to confine prostitution to the capital's zones of Alfama, Bairro Alto and Mouraria, where the punter would find the infamous *casas de meia-porta* [houses with a half-door] or *aventais de madeira* [wooden aprons].[9] These legal whorehouses — also known as *casas de fado* [Fado houses] — would not be outlawed until 1963.[10]

The Constitution that inaugurated the Estado Novo came into force in 1933. Shortly after the first wave of success of Marceneiro's 'A Casa da Mariquinhas', Salazar's regime and the Câmara Municipal de Lisboa (CML, Lisbon's City

---

[7] 'O Café de Camareiras', Gabriel de Oliveira / Alfredo Marceneiro; 'A Lucinda Camareira', Henrique Rêgo / Alfredo Marceneiro; 'Encontrei a Marcelina', João de Freitas / Fado Mouraria; 'A Casa da Mariquinhas', Silva Tavares / Alfredo Marceneiro. Sucena comments (p. 121) that by 1926, the last of the *cafés de camareiras*, *Boémia*, on Rua da Madelena near the Poço do Borratém, had closed. For more on the *cafés de camareiras*, see Colvin, *The Reconstruction of Lisbon*, pp. 85–87.
[8] Vítor Duarte Marceneiro, *Recordar Alfredo Marceneiro* (Lisbon: Editora Portuguesa de Livros, 1995) and *Alfredo Marceneiro... os fados que ele cantou* (Lisbon: Clássica Editora, 2001) for more on the biography and music of Marceneiro from the perspective of his grandson (*fadista*, Alfredo Duarte Jr's son).
[9] Sucena (p. 118) signals Article VIII of the *Carta Constitucional*.
[10] Ibid, p. 121.

Hall) would initiate urbanization projects — that would endure with the dictatorship — designed to bring progress to Lisbon's impoverished neighbourhoods.
The Minister of Public Works, Duarte Pacheco's plans for expanding Lisbon to
its northern suburbs (1938) would be carried out by Faria da Costa, upon the
former's accidental death in 1943. Under Faria da Costa's guidance, the CML
would level the western half of the Mouraria — corresponding to the present-day
Largo de Martim Moniz — and aim its wrecking balls at Alfama and the eastern
or Alta Mouraria, the birthplace of Maria Severa and the cradle of the Fado.

Nevertheless, Marceneiro's Fado would be a hit throughout the twentieth
century; and even in the early twenty-first, 'A Casa da Mariquinhas' is as present
in the repertoire of Fado fans as it was in the 1930s. The song's enduring success
is due in part to Marceneiro's live and recorded interpretations of the Fado,
and to the fact that 'A Casa da Mariquinhas' would inspire eleven ballads that
cannibalized the original Fado's lyrical motifs, themes, and, at times, its metre.
The later songs tell the story of the brothel's demise when Mariquinhas's house
is turned into a pawnshop, and the travels and disenchantments of the song's
protagonist, the Madam Mariquinhas. As a result, Lisbon's oral and recorded
underground *cancioneiro popular* archives the evolution and destruction of the
mythic bordello and — as half of the posterior verses set the whorehouse in the
Mouraria — the simultaneous surrender of Lisbon's traditions to the aesthetics
of progress, incarnate in the CML's demolition of the Baixa Mouraria.

Following Silva Tavares's detailed description of the interior of Mariquinhas's
brothel, Linhares Barbosa wrote the *fado corrido*, 'O Leilão', which chronicles the
auctioning of the closed whorehouse to a pawnbroker. In the second song, the
narrator goes to the Mouraria to discover the fate of the house and to question
Mouraria residents, o Chico do Cachené and Rosa Maria, about the auction.
He learns that Chico managed to salvage the guitar from the parlour and some
insignificant knick-knacks, but that 'Até das próprias janelas | Venderam-lhe as
tabuinhas' [They even sold the shutters | Right off the very windows]. Carlos
Conde wrote the third song in the cycle, the *fado mouraria*, 'Já Sabem da
Mariquinhas', which narrates the story of Mariquinhas's release from prison in
Cacilhas, after her brothel is closed. The narrator meets up with Mariquinhas,
Chico and Rosa Maria in the Cais do Sodré. Mariquinhas takes the guitar that
Chico has rescued from the auction but leaves behind the wooden shutters (that
were auctioned off with the house in the second song). In 'Depois do Leilão', the
narrator visits Mariquinhas's house, now Perdigão's pawnshop, to discover that
the house had been looted and despoiled of its 'velho bricabraque' [old bric-a-
brac], and that the neighbours — fearful that the neighbourhood urbanization
projects will force them to sell their homes — remember fondly the era when the
absent shutters 'falavam mais de amor' [spoke more of love].[11] In Alberto Janes's
adapted *fado corrido*, 'Vou Dar de Beber à Dor', the narrator visits Perdigão's
pawn shop — now presided over by an effeminate man — trying to find the

---

[11] 'Depois do Leilão', Linhares Barbosa / Alfredo Marceneiro.

shutters that have disappeared; the ensuing narration describes the pawn-shop, contrasting the coldness of its transactions to the warmth of Mariquinhas's business.[12] In 'A Fuga da Mariquinhas', the prostitute hires a donkey from a Gypsy in the Mouraria, and flees the capital up to Porto, where she will live in the shadow of the Cathedral.[13] In 'O Casino da Mariquinhas', Mariquinhas's house is but a memory of the 'vistosas tabuinhas' [remarkable shutters], for the neighbours who have all fled to Avenida da Liberdade as the Mouraria is turned to rubble.[14] Even Mariquinhas moves to Parque Mayer, sings at the Teatro Vitória, and dreams of performing at the Casino in Estoril. 'Vou Dar de Beber à Alegria' appropriates the cadence and melody of Alberto Janes's 'Vou Dar de Beber à Dor'; in this Fado, the narrator returns to Mariquinhas's house to find the shutters back on the windows, and an older, heavier Mariquinhas who has moved back to the Mouraria.[15] In 'A Senhora Mariquinhas', Mariquinhas has died and gone to heaven. No sooner is she dead than her neighbours malign her; they sack her house, taking her furniture and even objects of mere sentimental value, like her guitar, lace doilies, and the flowers and plants outside have wilted and dried up.[16] At her wake, Mariquinhas lies dead in a coffin made out of her house's shutters. However, in 'A Morte da Mariquinhas', the prostitutes and the same neighbours who had gossiped about them join together in mourning as Mariquinhas is carried away in a coffin, again made of her house's shutters.[17] In 'O Testamento da Mariquinhas', after the death of the brothel owner, there is a public reading of her will, in which she has left her guitar to God, her shawl to the Fado, and her shutters to the Mouraria (the very shutters that had been sold, abandoned, and converted into the prostitute's coffin).[18] Silva Tavares returns to write 'Cinquenta Anos Depois', in which an old man and his young wife live in Mariquinhas's former house.[19] The shutters are gone. And the guitar? 'Nem raça'. The wife spends most of her time in front of the mirror or in front of the bare window, thus provoking the nosy neighbours to speculate that the house may turn back into the brothel or a casa da Mariquinhas.

The motif of the wooden shutters that appears in the first twelve Fados in the Mariquinhas cycle assumes a covertly critical role as it signals the contrast between the discretion of a nineteenth-century Lisbon and a seemingly immodest capital of the twentieth. Rather, the absence of the humble architectural detail of the shutters on Estado Novo apartment buildings draws our attention to the Fado's proposed nostalgia in its eulogy to the homes of the past that were so prevalent in Lisbon's working-class neighbourhoods.

---

[12] 'Vou Dar de Beber à Dor', Alberto Janes.
[13] 'A Fuga da Mariquinhas', António Torre da Guia / Fado Mouraria. Torre da Guia also wrote 'A Resurreição da Mariquinhas', in which Mariquinhas dies upon her return from Porto to Lisbon.
[14] 'O Casino da Mariquinhas', Paulo Conde / Fado Mouraria.
[15] 'Vou Dar de Beber à Alegria', Hermínia Silva / Alberto Janes.
[16] 'A Senhora Mariquinhas', Sebastião Custódio Duarte.
[17] 'A Morte da Mariquinhas', Maria Manuela Mota / Paulo de Carvalho.
[18] 'O Testamento da Mariquinhas', Lopes Víctor / Alfredo Marceneiro.
[19] 'Cinquenta Anos Depois', Silva Tavares.

Furthermore, as the window and the front door of the poor Lisbon house have been contextualized in twentieth-century Fado lyrics as points of commerce in negotiating the transactions of freelance prostitution, the loci also serve as indicators of a resident's discretion; rather, appearing in a window or a doorway connotes the loose morals and propensity toward gossip on the part of one dweller; a closed or shuttered window confirms the decency and humility of another. Júlio Dantas's 'Novo Fado da Severa (Rua do Capelão)' equates the front steps to a prostitute's home with the entry to her bed and her heart: 'Tenho um degrau no meu leito | Que foi feito p'ra ti somente | Ó meu amor sobe-o com jeito | Se o meu coração te sente | Fica-me aos saltos no peito' [I have steps leading up to my bed | That were made just for you | Oh, my love, climb them carefully | If my heart should sense that you're near | It will skip a beat].[20] In 'Maria da Cruz' an innocent village woman loses her way when her shepherd boyfriend cheats on her, and she ends up as a prostitute in a doorway in the Mouraria: 'Desiludida do seu amor a Maria | Deixou o lar e perdida | Veio cair desfalecida | Num portal da Mouraria' [Disenchanted with her love | Maria left home and lost her way | She collapsed in a faint | In a doorway in the Mouraria].[21]

Nineteenth-century Inspector of Health in Lisbon, Francisco Inácio dos Santos Cruz, recommends that the authorities should 'prohibir [as prostitutas] de estar ás janellas em taes posiçoens, nem as mesmas conservar estando ás portas das ruas [...] os regulamentos devem também ordenar, que as suas janellas estejão sempre fechadas, e com cortinas por dentro das vidraças, ou com jelozias' [prohibit [the prostitutes] from adopting such attitudes at the windows, or remaining standing at the street doors [...] the regulations should also direct that their windows always be closed, and with curtains inside the widows, or with blinds].[22] In her book about late-eighteenth-century Lisbon, Suzanne Chantal comments on the prostitutes of the Bairro Alto and Mouraria who, at night, 'mantinham-se à janela e os seus ademanes eram bem explícitos' [stood in their windows making explicit gestures] and who 'dormia[m] durante o dia inteiro por detrás das suas gelosias de ripas' [spent the day sleeping behind their jalousie blinds].[23]

But as the CML demolishes the Mouraria, in line with its plans to supplant the emblematic neighbourhood of nineteenth-century prostitution with a more progressive, cleaner neighbourhood in the historic heart of the capital, the state's architectural blueprint of modern living clashes with age-old concepts of privacy and decency in an urban home. The shutters on nineteenth-century townhouses in Lisbon not only allowed Lisboners to close the noises of the city out of their living rooms, but also they served as reminders to the city that it should not be a witness to the goings-on in those very houses.

---

[20]   'Novo Fado da Severa (Rua do Capelão)', Júlio Dantas / Frederico de Freitas.
[21]   'Maria da Cruz', Amadeu do Vale / Frederico Valério.
[22]   Francisco Inácio dos Santos Cruz, *Da prostituição na cidade de Lisboa* (Porto: n.pub., 1841), p. 251.
[23]   Suzanne Chantal, *A vida quotidiana em Portugal ao tempo do terramoto* (Lisbon: Livros do Brasil, n.d. [*c.* 1965]), pp. 254–55.

Nevertheless, the engineers of Lisbon's Estado Novo-era make-over had deferred to French architects for its aesthetic cues — much like urban planners dating back to the late eighteenth-century Pombaline reconstruction of the Baixa. However, more liberal, northern European notions of domestic privacy came into conflict with Portuguese pudency on the balconies of *estado-novista* housing developments. And deep-seated native modesty goes out the window, literally, as the private quarters are exposed to the city streets.[24]

Varandinhas, or tiny wrought iron balconies large enough to hold a couple of plants or an air-conditioning unit, have been a common feature on the façades of Lisbon townhouses since the early twentieth century. Many nineteenth-century private homes and apartments, built in a Parisian style, had *sacadas* [limestone windowsills] contained by wooden guardrails that allowed the inhabitants to peer out of their tall French doors to see what was going on in the streets. In António Lopes Ribeiro's comedy film, 'A Vizinha do Lado' (1945), two neighbours fall in love during their flirtations, while peeking out of their tall windows at 13 Rua Castilho.[25] Pombaline houses in the Baixa and the Chiado have small fenced-in ledges big enough to step onto. And in Islamic Lixbuna, some houses had closed, latticed balconies that permitted Moslem women to keep vigil over the streets without the risk of strangers seeing them.[26]

But as Art-Deco buildings of the 1930s make their transition into Estado Novo monoliths of the 1940s to 1960s, the Portuguese *varandinhas* grow into full balconies and almost terraces. As a consequence, the half door with two windowpanes yields to wider four-paned glass doors and exposed windows. However, a stroll through Lisbon in pleasant weather, even during the summer, reveals the Portuguese recalcitrance to living private domestic moments outdoors; or rather, their rejection of the balcony. Apart from tourists at *pensões* [boarding houses] and office workers taking smoking breaks, few Lisboners spend time on their balconies. Furthermore, many owners of mid- to late twentieth-century houses have installed 'iron curtains', metal exterior blinds that isolate the indoors from the outdoors; and others have closed off their balconies by converting them into insulated indoor pantries with frosted windows.[27]

[24]   Keil Amaral, p. 23, speculates that inhabitants of southern European countries understand the dangers of the sun.
[25]   The building used in the film has since been demolished and replaced with a simple, white, cubical annex to the Hotel Altis. However, directly across Rua Rosa Araújo, at 15 Rua Castilho, are the ruins of a replica of 13 Rua Castilho, built by the same architect. It is interesting that the ground floor apartments at the ruins of 15 Rua Castilho still have wooden shutters. I lived in the third-floor apartment at 15 Rua Castilho during summers between 2000 and 2005, when the CML compelled the renters to leave so that the city could repossess the house and reconstruct its interior. At present, the building is a boarded-up ruin, and behind the shutters on the ground floor is a brick wall to keep out squatters.
[26]   José Luís de Matos, *Lisboa islâmica* (Lisbon: Instituto Camões, 1999), p. 18.
[27]   Kimberly DaCosta Holton, *Performing Folklore: Ranchos Folclóricos from Lisbon to Newark* (Bloomington: Indiana University Press, 2005), pp. 118–20, tells an anecdote about her stay at a relative's apartment in Lisbon, during which she left her windows and curtains open day and night. Her hostess often went into the room during the day to close the windows and the curtains, and eventually another relative intervened to warn her to keep her windows shut if she wanted to stay in the apartment.

In the Fados of the Mariquinhas cycle, the shutters that characterized brothels by their need to keep eyewitnesses at bay signal not only a nostalgic throwback to the context of the sordid nineteenth-century Mouraria, but also they appeal to a Portuguese sense of decorum regarding public and private life. Thus, the reappearance of the shutters to establish distance from gossipy neighbours, as artefacts to be sold off independently of the house, as symbols of the tender moments that occur behind them, as spare wood for a coffin, and as a legacy to be left to the Mouraria, constitutes a criticism of the CML's, and by association, the Estado Novo's approach to urbanization. That is, while the regime continues to demolish characteristic Portuguese houses, the Mariquinhas cycle protests at the very demolitions by redeeming the utility of the traditional Lisbon home. In its redemption of tradition, the Fados recognize the failure of the Regime to impose a seemingly cosmopolitan aesthetics on the Portuguese people.

However, the Fado is clever in its use of rhetoric to mask its subversive ambitions. Also, by appropriating the Regime's discourse on family values, the Fado turns the tables on the Estado Novo by placing the family at odds with the government's solutions to housing in Lisbon.

Family values in a whorehouse? Not exactly...

Whereas Silva Tavares's original Fado, 'A Casa da Mariquinhas', only hints at the fact that Mariquinhas is a prostitute — in its allusions to the shutters and Mariquinhas's nosy neighbours who peek in 'p'ra ver o que lá se passa' [to see what's going on there] — its description of the brothel is careful to avoid sensationalistic characterizations of a sordid atmosphere. Alfredo Marceneiro's doll's house re-creation of Silva Tavares's description of Mariquinhas's house is testament to a clean, relatively wholesome dwelling. Other than photographic vignettes of women in various stages of undress, posed in stencilled-in open windows, the house conforms to the image of the *casa portuguesa*. The house is a replica of a two-storey late eighteenth-, early nineteenth-century house, with half shutters on the ground-floor front windows and red velvet cushioning atop to simulate a clay roof which opens up to reveal a second floor where the bedrooms are. The rooms in the house are decorated with simple bourgeois furniture of the early twentieth century; the walls are papered and the windows have curtains; nothing is in decay, the rooms are tidy; and a bottle of sweet-almond oil is prominent in the kitchen: testament that the house is clean.[28]

Mariquinhas's house is not the filthy *casa de alcouce* [whorehouse] 'das ruas mais retiradas da cidade [...] em lojas nojentas de casas miseráveis' [located on the city's most secluded streets [...] in nauseating store fronts of miserable houses] that Santos Cruz describes in his report on prostitution in

---

[28] 'A Casa da Mariquinhas': Silva Tavares / Alfredo Marceneiro, 'Limpa as mobílias | Com óleo de amêndoa doce' [Mariquinhas cleans her furniture | With sweet almond oil]. Youtube, 'Alfredo Marceneiro — O leilão da casa da Mariquinhas', <http://www.youtube.com/watch?v=LHGTLmGi7U4> [accessed 24 July 2011]. In a televised interview (1969), Marceneiro gives a tour of the doll's house which he says he had built fifteen years earlier.

the Bairro Alto and the Mouraria of the nineteenth century.[29] Neither is it
Severa's childhood home, as described in Júlio Dantas's early twentieth-century
interpretation of the shanties that constituted a nineteenth-century Mouraria
brothel in his novel, A Severa (1901), where the legendary Rua Suja [Rua do
Capelão], 'com o seu ar triste de Mercado humano [...] morria antes do cantar
do galo, como uma grande chaga que se envergonha do Sol' [with its sad air
of a flesh market [...] died before cock-crow like a big lesion ashamed of the
sun].[30] Nor is it characteristic of what remains of the mid-twentieth-century
demolition of the western half of the Mouraria: 'O pitoresco que por aqui
existe está revestido de negrume e seria forçado classificar isto de interessante:
andares de ressalto, casas baixas, sombrias, viveiros de gente pobre' [Anything
picturesque in these parts is covered with soot and one would be hard pressed
to classify it as interesting: second floors jutting out of small sombre houses,
crowded with poor people].[31]

Silva Tavares's 'A Casa da Mariquinhas' and Alfredo Marceneiro's doll's house
maquette of the whorehouse that re-creates the former's description thwart our
expectations of what a Lisbon brothel should be. From the outside and within,
the details of Mariquinhas's house reflect the decency and discretion of an early
twentieth-century bourgeois Lisbon home, as it conforms to the prescription
of the Portuguese house. Whilst the audience of the Fado, not to mention the
admirers of Marceneiro's doll's house, are aware of the tolerated acts that take
place in Mariquinhas's house, they must use their imagination — just like the
murmuring neighbours — to condemn the brothel for its sordid atmosphere.

Since the lyrics to Linhares Barbosa's 'O Leilão', Alfredo Marceneiro's 'A
Menina do Mirante', and Silva Tavares's 'A Casa da Mariquinhas' and 'Cinquenta Anos Depois' are displayed prominently in Marceneiro's doll's house,
we are obliged to re-examine the songs of the Mariquinhas cycle in order to
understand the persistence and relevance of Silva Tavares's original lyrics in
subverting the official memory of Lisbon prostitution and of the Mouraria
brothel as a means to question the state's erasure of popular history; rather, the
futile censorship of urban myths that do not promote the regime's notion of a
progressive capital.[32]

[29] Santos Cruz, p. 164.
[30] Dantas, A Severa, p. 17.
[31] Norberto de Araújo, Peregrinações em Lisboa III (Lisbon: Vega, 1992), p. 68.
[32] 'A Menina do Mirante', Henrique Rêgo / Alfredo Marceneiro. Vieira Nery, pp. 219–20, characterizes
António Ferro's vision of the Secretariado da Propaganda Nacional (SPN, Ministry of National
Propaganda) as 'um aparelho de produção ideológica e cultural que promova activamente uma visão
do mundo consentânea com estes princípios: fortemente autoritária, hiper-nacionalista, católica
ultramontana, ruralista e portanto marcadamente anti-parlamentar e anti-liberal, contrária ao
cosmopolitismo modernista, desconfiada dos efeitos potencialmente desmoralizadores e descarac-
terizadores da urbanização e da industrialização' [an ideological and cultural production machine
that promotes actively a vision in keeping with the following principles: strongly authoritarian,
hyper-nationalistic, ultramontane Catholic, ruralist, and therefore distinctly anti-parliamentary
and anti-liberal, opposed to modernist cosmopolitanism, hostile to the potentially demoralizing
and dehumanizing effects of urbanization and industrialization]. Artur Portela, Salazarismo e

In 1980, Hermínia Silva recorded a new interpretation of Alberto Janes's 'Vou Dar de Beber à Dor', titled, 'Vou Dar de Beber à Alegria'. Silva combines her talent for singing complicated narrative in outdated *fadista* slang and elaborates her sense of humour through an intercalated *fado falado* that serves like a theatrical chorus to update the audience on Mariquinhas's return to her house, while paying homage to the tradition of the Mariquinhas songs.

Hermínia Silva had pioneered the great era of twentieth-century Fado: she had participated in the great *retiros* of the 1930s, and had owned two successful Fado houses, one in Lisbon's Bairro Alto (O Solar da Hermínia) and the other in the Ribatejo town of Alhandra (O Retiro da Hermínia). She brings hope to a cycle of songs that prophesied the Fado's disappearance in the changing Portuguese values, values that favoured progress over tradition.[33] As the wrecking balls had already turned away from the Mouraria before the 25 April Revolution, and those buildings that had escaped demolition were relatively safe, the Mouraria could begin to face its future. Hermínia's toast to happiness rings in a new era marked by a return to Fado that will result in UNESCO's protection of the Fado as Intangible Cultural Heritage, and the CML's eventual rehabilitation of the Mouraria, centred around its only tourist attraction, the house at 36 Rua do Capelão, where Maria Severa lived and worked as a prostitute in the 1820s:

> Foi ontem mesmo que passei
> À Mouraria onde vivia a Mariquinhas
> E como antigamente
> Lá na rua que vai em frente
> Espreitei as famosas tabuinhas
> Desde a velha Rua da Palma
> Eu não vi nenhuma alma
> Que recordasse a Mariquinhas
> E lá na Rua do Calvário
> Eu bebi umas ginjinhas.
>
> [Just yesterday I passed by
> The Mouraria where Mariquinhas used to live
> And just like in the old days
> On the street that runs in front
> I glimpsed the famous shutters
> From the old Rua da Palma
> I didn't see a single soul
> Who remembered Mariquinhas
> And over on Rua do Calvário
> I drank some *ginjinhas*.][34]

artes plásticas (Lisbon: Instituto de Cultura e Língua Portuguesa, 1982), understands that beyond the apparent goal of fighting anti-social ideas, Ferro's SPN hoped to invent Salazar and a Salazarist mythology.

[33] Víctor Duarte Marceneiro, *Recordar Hermínia Silva* (Lisbon: Grafispaço, 2004), for more information about the *fadista*.

[34] The CML and Programa de ação QREN Mouraria have restored Severa's house. On 13 July 2013, the Museu do Fado opened the Casa de Severa, a cultural space devoted to Fado.

Acção Realista Portuguesa:
An Organization of the Anti-Liberal Right, 1923–26

Ernesto Castro Leal

Universidade de Lisboa

Introduction

The essential reasoning of the Portuguese anti-liberal right questioned the individualist, utilitarian and relativist logic of liberalism, democracy and republicanism, seen by them as tending towards the dissolution of the 'traditional constitution' of the Portuguese nation, which in turn was seen to incorporate an eternal imaginary based on historical providentialism, a foundational mythology, the dominant position of the Catholic religion in the moral sphere, and a political formula of a strong state or a corporative organization.

Within the field of the nationalist and organicist right, traditionalist nationalism was dominant, despite its coexisting with revolutionary nationalism, less widely accepted. Traditionalist nationalism was discussed in the following way by Fernando Pessoa:

> o nacionalismo tradicionalista, que é o que faz consistir a substância da nacionalidade em qualquer ponto do seu passado, e a vitalidade nacional na continuidade histórica com esse ponto do passado. Diversos são os critérios com que se pode buscar esse ponto do passado, mas, seja qual for o critério que se empregue, a essência do *processus* é a mesma [...].[1]

> [traditionalist nationalism, which sees the substance of nationality as lying at some point in the past, and the national vitality in the historical continuity with that point in the past. There are various criteria for locating that point in the past, but whatever criterion is employed, the essence of the *processus* is the same [...].]

The nationalism of the anti-liberal right, being profoundly critical of the Enlightenment, rationalism and materialism, evoked the myth of national foundation by D. Afonso Henriques (and the alleged appearance of Christ at the battle of Ourique), but based itself on the reworking of the myth of the national refoundation by D. Nuno Álvares Pereira (as hero and saint), by the exemplary blossoming of patriotism and spiritualist nationalism to 'refundir-se, sem desfiguração, a imagem original de Portugal' [for the original image of Portugal

[1]   Fernando Pessoa, *Da República, 1910–1935* (Lisbon: Ática, 1979), p. 223.

Portuguese Studies vol. 30 no. 1 (2014), 47–66

to be refounded, without disfigurement], as the monarchist constitutionalist, Carlos Malheiro Dias, declared in 1924, with a great impact on the anti-liberal right. He went on to say:

> Nacionalismo não é sinónimo de isolamento, mas defesa legítima contra a decadência do espírito nacional [...]. A nossa forma não é a armadura do Cid ou a de Joana d'Arc, mas a de Nun'Álvares. Não sei de nações robustas que não se tenham criado ao peito do nacionalismo.[2]

> [Nationalism is not synonymous with isolation, but a legitimate defence against the decline of the national spirit [...]. Our model is not the armour of El Cid or of Joan of Arc, but that of Nun' Álvares. I know of no healthy nations that were not nursed at the bosom of nationalism.]

Our aim in the article is to analyse the milestones in the social and political ideology and the public dynamic of the Acção Realista Portuguesa, an organization of the anti-liberal right. Under the leadership of the intellectual Alfredo Pimenta,[3] with the participation of António Cabral (former minister under the monarchy), Ernesto Gonçalves[4] (editor of the journal *Acção Realista*, 1924–26), João Ameal[5] and Luís Chaves (joint editors of *Acção Realista*, April–August 1926) and Luís Chaves alone (as editor of the daily *A Voz Nacional*, December 1925–March 1926), it contributed to the diversity of the nationalist scene in Portugal between 1923 and 1926. It embodied an integralist and monarchist ideal — Integralist Nationalism — in obedience to D. Manuel II as representative of the Portuguese royal family, and a number of its most significant leaders came to occupy important regional or national positions in the Salazar dictatorship of the Estado Novo, some in conformity with it, some in tension with it. Those who participated included Alfredo Pimenta,[6] Caetano Beirão, João Ameal, Fernando Campos, António Eça de Queiroz, João Pinto da Costa Leite (Lumbrales), Ernesto Gonçalves, Alfredo de Freitas Branco (Visconde do Porto da Cruz), Bento Caldas and Luís da Câmara Pina.

---

[2] C. [Carlos] Malheiro Dias, *Exortação à Mocidade* (Porto: Litografia Nacional, 1924), p. 19.
[3] For a history of the life and thought of Alfredo Pimenta, cf. Alfredo Pimenta, *A evolução dum pensamento (auto-biografia filosófica): lição proferida na Biblioteca Geral da Universidade de Coimbra, em 6 de Maio de 1935* (Coimbra: Imprensa da Universidade, 1935); Maria Tereza Pimenta, 'Cronologia da vida e da obra de Alfredo Pimenta', *Boletim de Trabalhos Históricos*, 34 (1983), 44–64; António José de Brito, 'O pensamento de Alfredo Pimenta', *Futuro presente*, 21/22 (1985), 9–24; Ernesto Castro Leal, 'O tempo de Alfredo Pimenta: mitologia política e nacionalismo entre a Primeira República e o Estado Novo', *Revista de Guimarães*, 111 (2001), 103–43; Barroso da Fonte, *Alfredo Pimenta: da praxis libertária à doutrinação nacionalista* (Guimarães: Cidade Berço, 2005).
[4] Emanuel Janes, *Nacionalismo e nacionalistas na Madeira nos anos trinta (1928–1936)* (Funchal: Centro de Estudos de História do Atlântico/Secretaria Regional do Turismo e Cultura, 1997), pp. 83–103.
[5] António Francisco Figueiredo Cordeiro Lopes, *O pensamento e a acção de João Ameal: um percurso antimoderno, entre o Integralismo e o Salazarismo (1917–1934)* (Lisbon: Faculdade de Letras da Universidade de Lisboa, 1995).
[6] Cf. *Salazar e Alfredo Pimenta: correspondência, 1931–1950 (Prefácio de Manuel Braga da Cruz)* (Lisbon: Verbo, 2008).

At the Paris Dynastic Pact of 17 April 1922, liberal constitutionalist monarchists (represented by Aires de Ornelas e Vasconcelos, lieutenant to D. Manuel II) and traditionalist anti-liberal monarchists (represented by D. Miguel Vaz de Almada, delegated by D. Aldegundes de Bragança, daughter of D. Miguel I, Countess of Bardi, and lieutenant to D. Duarte Nuno) agreed to recognize D. Manuel II as the legitimate representative of the Portuguese royal family. However, on 4 May 1922, the Junta Central of Integralismo Lusitano declared itself against the Pact, suspended its political activity, and retreated into the doctrinaire boundaries of the journal *Nação Portuguesa*, 'revista de cultura nacionalista' [journal of nationalist culture].

Within that ideological camp, the exception to this ideological retreat was exemplified by its monarchist syndicalist component, influenced by the integralist theorizing of Charles Maurras, and the syndicalism of Georges Valois,[7] who grouped themselves around the *A Revolução*, 'jornal monárquico-sindicalista' [monarchist syndicalist newspaper]. Also involved was Francisco Rolão Preto,[8] who had made connections with the Centro do Nacionalismo Lusitano, led by João de Castro Osório, which stood for a nationalist dictatorship with fascist overtones.[9]

The Paris Pact would be repudiated in November 1925, leading to a renewal in political activity by the Junta Central of Integralismo Lusitano, from 12 March 1926, but that did not translate into a significant organized intervention. Integralismo Lusitano remained united around a doctrinaire ideological and cultural circle, despite the participation of some of its members in the revolution of 28 May 1926 at the side of General Manuel Gomes da Costa, including Manuel Múrias, who belonged to the small initial group that set Gomes da Costa out on the road to Braga with the aim of setting up a revolutionary pole in the north of Portugal, and Corporal Luís Charters de Azevedo (son of the Viscount of S. Sebastião), who was the Leiria district delegate for Acção Realista Portuguesa.

Origins of Integralist Nationalism: Integralists Loyal to D. Manuel II

The segment of Integralismo Lusitano that pledged dynastic loyalty to D. Manuel II wished to advance its political and organizational autonomy, creating the Acção Tradicionalista Portuguesa, between July 1921 and May 1922, and the Acção Realista Portuguesa, between December 1923 and December 1926.

---

[7] Eugen Weber, *L'Action française* (Paris: Stock, 1926); Zeev Sternhell, *La Droite révolutionnaire, 1885–1914: les origines françaises du fascisme* (Paris: Seuil, 1978); Raoul Girardet, *Le Nationalisme français: anthologie, 1871–1914* (Paris: Seuil, 1983).

[8] Cecília Barreira, 'Sindicalismo e integralismo: o jornal "A Revolução" (1922–23)', *Análise Social*, 67/68/69 (1981), 827–38; João Medina, *Salazar e os fascistas. Salazarismo e Nacional-Sindicalismo: a história dum conflito, 1932–1935* (Amadora: Bertrand, 1979); António Costa Pinto, *Os Camisas Azuis: ideologia, elites e movimentos fascistas em Portugal (1914–1945)* (Lisbon: Estampa, 1994).

[9] João de Castro [Osório], *A revolução nacionalista* (Lisbon: Edição do Autor, 1922). Cf. António Costa Pinto, 'O fascismo e a crise da Primeira República: os nacionalistas lusitanos (1923–25)', *Penélope*, 3 (1989), 43–62; Ernesto Castro Leal, *António Ferro: espaço político e imaginário social (1918–1932)* (Lisbon: Cosmos, 1994), pp. 113–20.

The theoretical framework of these monarchist political organizations was provided mainly by Alfredo Pimenta, an intellectual who had always rejected liberal individualism, both during his flirtation with anarchism and during his affiliations to republicanism and monarchism. Prior to the Acção Realista Portuguesa he had been involved in the ephemeral Acção Tradicionalista Portuguesa, run by himself and Luís Chaves, in whose *Manifesto-Programa*, dated 25 July 1921, could to be found still some ideological legacy of liberal monarchism.

On 20 October 1919, Integralismo Lusitano agreed to abandon its dynastic loyalty to D. Manuel II, and on 9 September 1920 it united with the Partido Legitimista (refounded in 1915, with the reappearance of the journal *A Nação*), which had gathered together traditionalist *miguelista* monarchists, loyal to D. Miguel's branch of the House of Bragança; this decision opened up the way for those sections of integralism still loyal to D. Manuel II to regroup politically and organizationally. And while Alfredo Pimenta was undoubtedly the ideologist of this camp, we should not forget the ethnologist Luís Chaves, who had also been a member, since 1921, of the Cruzada Nacional D. Nuno Álvares Pereira.[10]

According to a statement by Luís Chaves, he was the author of a proposal, presented at the end of July 1921, for the creation of a group called the Núcleo Integralista D. Manuel II, which evolved into the Acção Tradicionalista Portuguesa, a name more appealing to Alfredo Pimenta,[11] perhaps because it was related semantically to his inspiration, *Action Française*. Alfredo Pimenta drew up the *Manifesto-Programa*, signed by members of the Junta Directiva, namely Mateus da Graça de Oliveira Monteiro, Luís Rufino Chaves Lopes, Caetano Maria de Abreu Beirão, Alberto Ramires dos Reis and Alfredo Pimenta himself.[12] D. Manuel II would write from London that the political objectives of the group had his full approval and he hoped that 'uma tão inteligente orientação contribua de uma forma eficaz para acabar de vez com as divisões existentes na família monárquica' [such an intelligent approach would contribute in an efficient manner to ending once and for all the divisions within the monarchist family].[13]

While the founding document is clear as to the anti-liberal, anti-democratic and anti-parliamentary worldview of the principal promoters of Acção Tradicionalista Portuguesa, influenced by anti-democratic organicists such as Auguste Comte, Charles Maurras and Léon Daudet, it is not entirely explicit as to the solution to the political problem, where it recognizes the existence of political parties. They distanced themselves somewhat from the basic principles of Integralismo Lusitano, which they claimed not to question, in contrast to

[10]   Ernesto Castro Leal, *Nação e nacionalismos: a Cruzada Nacional D. Nuno Álvares Pereira e as origens do Estado Novo (1918–1938)* (Lisbon: Cosmos, 1999).
[11]   *Correio da Manhã*, 11 August 1921, p. 1.
[12]   *Correio da Manhã*, 28 July 1921, p. 1; *A Acção Tradicionalista Portuguesa*, 10 December 1921, pp. 5–8.
[13]   *A Acção Tradicionalista Portuguesa*, 10 December 1921, p. 3.

what would happen in 1924 at the start of the Acção Realista Portuguesa, when three leading members of Acção Tradicionalista Portuguesa were present, namely Alfredo Pimenta, Caetano Beirão and Luís Chaves.

This group put forward two objectives, which were stated on the covers of the only two numbers of the journal *A Acção Tradicionalista Portuguesa* (10 and 30 December 1921): 'A Acção Tradicionalista Portuguesa visa a unificação da Causa Monárquica' [Acção Tradicionalista Portuguesa aims for the unification of the Monarchist Cause], and 'O programa político da Acção Tradicionalista Portuguesa é a plataforma onde se podem encontrar todos os monárquicos antiliberais' [The political programme of Acção Tradicionalista Portuguesa is the platform on which all anti-liberal monarchists can meet]. Amongst the political ideas presented in the *Manifesto-Programa*, one finds the restoration of the Monarchy, with the King as central sovereign power, advised by a Council of State, and enjoying full powers in matters of diplomacy and defence. In relation to the Executive he would have the authority to freely nominate and dismiss ministers, who would be assisted by technical commissions, also nominated by the King, with the purpose of preparing laws.

The legislative power (the formal assembly) was to be based on the traditional Cortes, composed of two chambers: a Chamber of Deputies, elected by restricted suffrage (based on taxable wealth and technical aptitude), made up of two thirds recognized professions and one third political parties; and a Chamber of Peers, of which one part was nominated by the Crown and was hereditary, while the other was constituted of provincial procurators and representatives of the active corporations, and of the clergy, and could be dissolved by the King. The national representation was limited in its competence to matters of budgets and taxation, while the Chamber of Peers had the special function of modifying the Constitutional Statute.

In international affairs, they proposed maintaining and strengthening the alliance with the United Kingdom, making it the basis of Portugal's foreign policy, while also improving diplomatic ties with Spain and Brazil. In religious matters, they recognized the need to concede privileges to the Catholic Church, allowing it to choose freely the nature of its relations with the state — whether by maintaining its independence from the state or by entering into a concordat with it — and they were willing to defend the country's religious orders.

Social affairs were approached from an organicist perspective, harmonizing the 'interesse solidário' [shared interests] of capital and labour, with protection for syndicalism at the economic level, the defence of the 'interesses espirituais e morais' [spiritual and moral interests] of the workforce, and the development of technical schools at the primary, middle and higher levels. Finally, in administrative matters they favoured municipal institutions and the creation of provincial bodies, thereby rejecting the division into districts that had been in force since the legislation of 18 July 1835 (Rodrigo da Fonseca Magalhães) and enshrined in the Administrative Code of 31 December 1836 (Passos Manuel).

How, though, were they to reconcile their defence of a bicameral Cortes, where there was representation by political parties, with the integralist mould of the organic monarchy, traditionalist and anti-parliamentary? It seems to have been difficult, with Alfredo Pimenta arguing, in his text 'Palavras claras' that the existence of political parties as an integral part of the constitution during a century of liberalism meant that they should now be regarded as being amongst the 'elementos tradicionalistas do País' [traditionalist elements of the Country]. To refuse to recognize political parties, he said, ran the risk of leading them into a 'situação revolucionária' [revolutionary situation]. He summarized the essential political ideas of the Acção Tradicionalista Portuguesa thus:

> O nosso programa não é uma plataforma dada a liberais e antiliberalistas. Não. O nosso programa é o programa dos antiliberalistas que reconhecem a legitimidade de El-Rei D. Manuel [...]. Em todas alíneas, o nosso Programa é antiliberalista, essencialmente tradicionalista, e sistematicamente nacionalista [...]. Reconhece-se a existência dos partidos políticos, porque os partidos políticos são um facto. Reconhecer os factos não é transigir com os factos mas integrar-se neles.[14]

> [Our political programme is not a platform given to [both] liberals and anti-liberalists. Our programme is the programme of the anti-liberalists who recognize the legitimacy of our King, D. Manuel [...]. In every clause, our Programme is anti-liberalist, essentially traditionalist, and systematically nationalist [...]. It recognizes the existence of political parties because political parties are a fact. To recognize facts is not to make concessions to them, but to integrate oneself with them.]

Caetano Beirão would recall Italian fascism as the 'mais belo, mais alto exempo' [finest, highest example] of an anti-democratic regime; the fascists in Italy, he declared, had shown themselves to be 'verdadeiros nacionalistas, remando contra a maré-baixa dos tempos presentes' [true nationalists, rowing against the ebbing tide of the present times], and combatting the two dominant models of the 'vírus democrático — o bolchevismo bravo de Trotzky e de Lenine e o bolchevismo manso dum Briand ou dum Barthou' [democratic virus — the savage Bolshevism of Trotsky and Lenin and the tame Bolshevism of the likes of Briand and Barthou].[15] Dialogue with the fascist ideal was not supported by all integralists, who divided between the 'monarchists' and the 'mono-archists'. Fascism was seen as exemplary in that it proposed a transition from 'disorder' (a liberal democracy, whether monarchical or republican) towards a new 'order' (an organic, anti-liberal monarchy).

The Acção Tradicionalista Portuguesa aimed to develop a space for an ideological convergence of anti-liberal monarchists, between those who completely accepted the propositions of Integralismo Lusitano, for whom

[14]   Alfredo Pimenta, 'Palavras claras', A Acção Tradicionalista Portuguesa, 10 December 1921, pp. 11–12.
[15]   Caetano Beirão, 'A hora que passa', A Acção Tradicionalista Portuguesa, 10 December 1921, pp. 16–18.

nationalism preceded monarchism, and those who did not entirely accept their political programme — whether because they regarded the monarchy as taking precedence over nationalism, or because they rejected the reestablishment of the system of mortgaged property, or regionalism in art (the social function of art), or economic syndicalism (workers' unions, employers' unions, or mixed types). A group of students from Coimbra formed the Núcleo do Nacionalismo Integral, united around the journal *A Restauração*.

The apparently successful negotiations between the two branches of the Portuguese royal house (the Paris Pact of 17 April 1922) led to the dissolution of Acção Tradicionalista Portuguesa, announced by way of a public notice signed on 5 May 1922 by its Junta Directiva and by a representative of the Junta Central and the Junta Financeira.[16] This political group went on to approve an organizational structure (with a Junta Directiva, Junta Financeira, Junta Central, Delegações Provinciais, Juntas Municipais and Núcleos de Freguesia) in order to create a national membership network.

However, the confrontation between liberal and anti-liberal monarchists sharpened again from the beginning of 1923. Alfredo Pimenta actively re-emerged with his *Cartas Monárquicas* (no. 1 issued 15 January 1923), and gained some prominence with his address on *As Bases da Monarquia Futura*, delivered on 27 May 1923, in Lisbon, at the headquarters of the Juventudes Monárquicas Conservadoras. This organization had links with Fidelino Figueiredo, who edited the journal *Portugália*, 'revista de cultura, tradição e renovação nacional' [journal of culture, tradition and national renovation] (no. 1 issued October 1925), which belonged to the Conselho Director Central of the Juventudes Monárquicas Conservadoras. In his speech, Alfredo Pimenta insisted on the renewal of the monarchist ideal through integralist principles — an organic, traditionalist and anti-parliamentary monarchy — and criticized the basis of the liberal state, whether monarchist or republican. He also described the present position of organic nationalist activity and made a defence of economic and professional syndicalism, declaring that a monarchical regime would only be viable — and this is relevant here — if it were imposed in a violent manner.

Affirmation of Integralist Nationalism: Ideology, Elites and Dynamic

The anti-liberal monarchist ideal, in its integralist nationalist variant loyal to D. Manuel II, re-emerged towards the end of 1923 and reached a significant audience, from the beginning of 1924, around Acção Realista Portuguesa, heavily influence by *Action Française*. Just three months after the formation of this group, Alfredo Pimenta wrote:

> Toda a gente sabe em Portugal a simpatia que temos pelo movimento e pelas doutrinas da *Action Française*, e esta não o ignora [...]. Acompanhamos

---

[16]   *Correio da Manhã*, 6 May 1922, p. 2.

esse movimento desde 1906, e não temos dúvida em confessar que muito devemos ao sr. Maurras como ao falecido Léon de Montesquion, na solução que o nosso espírito encontrou para alguns dos problemas políticos que o preocupavam [...].[17]

[Everyone in Portugal knows the sympathy we have toward the organization and the doctrines of *Action Française*, and they [themselves] are not unaware of it [...]. We have been following this organization since 1906, and we have no hesitation in admitting that we owe much to M. Maurras, as well as the late Léon de Montesquion, in the solution that our minds have found for some of the political problems that concerned him [...].]

In the consolidation phase of Acção Realista Portuguesa, António Cabral (a member of its Executive Commission and a former minister in liberal monarchist governments in 1905–06 and in 1908–09) mentioned *Action Française* in a speech delivered on 18 December 1924, which was reported as follows: '[...] referindo-se à acção actual da monarquia, combateu a sua passividade e afirmou que é pela política à maneira da *Action Française* que se conseguirá chegar à restauração, e perguntou porque é que vamos buscar tantos maus exemplos à França e não os bons' [referring to the present activity of the monarchy, he attacked its passivity and declared that it was through politics after the manner of *Action Française* that it would be possible to achieve restoration, and he asked why it was that we looked to France for so many bad examples, and not for good ones].[18]

In discussing the emergent dictatorships, Cabral also made allusion to General Miguel Primo da Rivera and the Spanish military dictatorship of 1923 as political examples for superseding the liberal state:

Se no dia 5 de Outubro de 1910, tivesse ido para a Rotunda, em vez de Machado Santos, representante da Maçonaria e da Carbonária, um Primo de Rivera, representante da Ordem e das Tradições — o 5 de Outubro teria sido um acto de solene patriotismo, não deixando, por isso, a Monarquia de 1910 de passar à História...[19]

[If on 5 October 1910, instead of Machado Santos, a representative of the Masonry and the Carbonária, there had gone to the Rotunda a man like Primo de Rivera, a representative of Order and Tradition — then the 5th October would have been an act of solemn patriotism, even though the Monarchy of 1910 would still have passed into History...]

Mussolini would receive the greatest panegyrics in the pages of the daily *Acção Realista*, in an unsigned text which also displays aspects of an ideological self-portrait of Alfredo Pimenta at that time. This makes it almost certain that he himself was the author of the text:

---

[17]   Alfredo Pimenta, 'O meu protesto', *Correio da Manhã*, 10 September 1923, p. 2.
[18]   *Acção Realista*, 1 January 1925, p. 19.
[19]   *Da Mensagem de 8 de Dezembro à Acção Realista Portuguesa* (Lisbon: Acção Realista Portuguesa, 1924), p. 3.

Mussolini é hoje a figura mais representativa da Contra-Revolução europeia. Vindo do campo do extremo revolucionarismo, o ditador italiano, abandonando as quimeras subversivas, conservou sempre o ímpeto voluntarioso, a varonilidade indómita, e o desdém por todos os preconceitos fossilizados. Quando revolucionário, Mussolini conheceu a íntima energia da vida social: acreditou a princípio que essa energia era a agitação rude, o cachoar revolucionário; mas as realidades italianas, num momento gravíssimo da sua Pátria, lançaram-no na grande estrada da Ordem e do Trabalho organizado. É por esse motivo que a política Mussoliniana vibra na trepidação de uma acção construtiva, e segue a ideia nítida duma sociedade solidária servindo um Estado forte [...].[20]

[Mussolini is today the most representative figure of the European Counter-Revolution. Coming from the camp of extreme revolutionism, the Italian dictator, abandoning subversive chimeras, has always retained his wilful impetus, his indomitable manliness, and his disdain for all fossilized preconceptions. As a revolutionary, Mussolini understood the vital energy of pubic activity: he believed at first that that energy was vulgar agitation, the revolutionary tumult; but Italian realities, at a very serious moment for his Fatherland, launched him on the high road of Order and organized Labour. It is for this reason that Mussolini's politics throb in trepidation for constructive action, and follow the clear notion of a united society serving a strong state [...].]

The integralist nationalists' critique of the dominant liberal monarchist logic governing the Conselho Superior Político of the Causa Monárquica culminated with the Lisbon Message, directed again at Aires de Ornelas, and symbolically dated 'no dia de N. Senhora da Conceição, Padroeira do Reino em 1923' [on the day of Our Lady of the Immaculate Conception, Patron of the Kingdom, 1923], i.e. 8 December. It began as a letter from Alfredo Pimenta addressed to D. Manuel II's lieutenant, but turned into a message signed initially by 435 monarchists: this was the immediate origin of the Acção Realista Portuguesa. This document set out to protest against the liberal orientation of the newspaper *Correio da Manhã*, the official daily of the Causa Monárquica, which ignored the fact that that organization 'é constituída por diversas correntes doutrinárias, umas, ligadas aos princípios do liberalismo democrático, outras, inspiradas nas modernas formas antiparlamentares e sindicalistas ou profissionais' [is composed of different doctrinal currents, some linked to the principles of democratic liberalism, others inspired by modern anti-parliamentary and syndicalist or professional models].[21]

The signatories, anti-liberal monarchists of that time, started by demanding the appearance of their political ideas in the said periodical, going on, on 16 January 1924, in another document delivered to Aires de Ornelas, to put

---

[20] *Acção Realista*, 31 July 1926, p. 1.
[21] *Carta ao Snr. Conselheiro Aires de Ornelas, Lugar-Tenente de Sua Majestade El-Rei* (Lisbon: Lucas, 1923); *Da Mensagem de 8 de Dezembro à Acção Realista Portuguesa* (Lisbon: Acção Realista Portuguesa, 1924).

forward the demand that they constitute a political force directly subordinated to it. The next day Aires de Ornelas, in reply to this demand, would confirm his authorization for the organization and propagation of the signatories' ideas within the Causa Monárquica.

This decision opened the way for holding a meeting, on 19 January 1924, of the signatories to the 8 December Message, at which an Organizing Commission, later to become the Executive Commission, for Acção Realista Portuguesa was elected. Its members were António Cabral, the Conde de Sucena (2nd Conde de Sucena, José Rodrigues de Sucena), the Visconde do Torrão, D. Rui Zarco da Câmara, Alfredo Pimenta, José Pedro Folque, Francisco Xavier Quintela, Ernesto Gonçalves and Caetano Beirão. Of these, the Visconde do Torrão, Rui da Câmara, Quintela and Folque were former militants in monarchist movements against the First Republic. On 29 January 1924 the following *Declaração de Doutrina* was be signed:

> A comissão organizadora da Acção Realista Portuguesa, dentro das atribuições que lhe foram conferidas pelos signatários da mensagem de 8 de Dezembro, declara que as suas doutrinas correspondem ao restabelecimento da Monarquia orgânica, tradicionalista e antiparlamentar que durante séculos fez glória a Portugal e que, pela sua essência nacionalista e positiva, é o único regime capaz de restituir a Nação aos seus destinos históricos.[22]

> [The organizing committee of Acção Realista Portuguesa, by virtue of the powers that were conferred on it by the signatories of the Message of 8 December, declares that its doctrines correspond to the re-establishment of the organic, traditionalist and anti-parliamentary Monarchy, which for centuries was the glory of Portugal, and which, by its nationalist and positive essence, is the only regime capable of restoring the Nation to its historical destiny.]

Article I of the Estatutos would lay out its ideological foundation, in the following way: 'A Acção Realista Portuguesa tem por fim propagar e defender o sistema de princípios políticos conhecido pela designação de "Nacionalismo Integral", até conseguir a instauração da Monarquia orgânica, tradicionalista e antiparlamentar' [Acção Realista Portuguesa has as its aim to advance and defend the system of political principles known as 'Integralist Nationalism', until it is able to install an organic, traditionalist and anti-parliamentary Monarchy].[23]

The Bases de Organização,[24] which would be expanded upon in the Estatutos, provided for the main structures: a Junta Directiva [Management Committee], Juntas Provinciais and Delegados [Provincial Committees and Branches], Juntas Municipais and Delegados [Municipal Committees and Branches], and Núcleos de Freguesia [Parish Cells]. The national coverage of Acção Realista Portuguesa would be provided for by a network of branches

---

[22] *Acção Realista*, 10 June 1924, p. 40.
[23] *Acção Realista*, 26 April 1926, p. 3.
[24] *Acção Realista*, 22 May 1924, p. 17.

(Beja, Braga, Bragança, Castelo Branco, Coimbra, Covilhã, Évora, Faro, Funchal, Guarda, Horta, Leiria, Lisbon, Portalegre, Porto, Viana do Castelo and Vila Real), the creation of various provincial and municipal committees, and academic committees in the Universities of Coimbra, Porto and Lisbon. A number of periodicals were also created, for example, *Acção Realista* (Lisbon), first as a journal (22 May 1924 to March and October 1926) and then as a daily (14 April 1926 to 13 August 1926), *A Voz Nacional* (Lisbon; 8 December 1925 to 8 March 1926), and *Acção Algarvia* (Silves). Furthermore, *A Realeza* (Vila Real) and *A Restauração* (Coimbra) were adopted as official organs, as were *Acção Académica* (Porto) and *O Município* (Setúbal).

At the end of 1924, in support of Acção Realista Portuguesa, the hero of the monarchist incursions of 1911–12, Henrique de Paiva Couceiro, began publication in *Acção Realista* of his 'Carta Aberta aos meus Amigos e Companheiros' [Open Letter to my Friends and Comrades] — a general political programme in which he addressed political, social and economic issues, as well as justice and defence. Publication continued over ten issues of the journal, from 1 November 1924 to 15 June 1925, and the letter would go on sale in its entirety, at eighty-two pages, under the imprint Edição da Acção Realista Portuguesa (the first volume of a Biblioteca de Estudos Nacionalistas). They acknowledged that such recognition represented a significant act of political complicity and a moral stimulus to the organization: 'a Acção Realista Portuguesa honra-se de o contar entre os seus melhores amigos' [Acção Realista Portuguesa is honoured to count him amongst its best friends].[25]

The historian Vasco Pulido Valente interpreted Couceiro's action in the following way:

> Depois de um longo silêncio, em 1924, Couceiro reapareceu com uma *Carta Aberta Aos Meus Amigos e Companheiros*. Este livro (na realidade, a separata de uma revista) anunciava uma reconciliação (entre ele próprio e o rei) e a criação de um novo grupo político, a *Acção Realista*, em que entrava a gente que sempre obedecera a D. Manuel, uma dissidência *integralista* e alguns velhos fiéis da 'Galiza', como Xavier Quintela, José Pedro Folque e Rui da Câmara. Para além de reiterar a natureza 'tradicional e antiparlamentar' da futura Monarquia, o livro tinha dois fins. Primeiro, explicar que D. Manuel não estava obrigado a restaurar a Carta, que jurara em 1908. E, segundo, garantir que, se ele, Couceiro, a restaurara no Porto em 1919, fora apenas por uma questão de oportunidade.[26]

> [After a long silence Couceiro reappeared, in 1924, with his *Open Letter to my Friends and Comrades*. This book (in reality an offprint from a journal) announced a reconciliation (between himself and the King) and the creation of a new political group, *Acção Realista*, which was joined by people who had always been loyal to D. Manuel, some dissident Integralists and a few faithful friends from 'Galicia', such as Xavier Quintela, José Pedro

[25] *Acção Realista*, 1 January 1925, p. 1.
[26] Vasco Pulido Valente, *Um herói português: Henrique Paiva Couceiro (1861–1944)* (Lisbon: Alêtheia, 2006), p. 144.

Folque and Rui da Câmara. As well as reiterating the 'traditional and anti-parliamentary' nature of the future monarchy, the book had two aims. First, to explain that D. Manuel was not obliged to restore the Charter that he had sworn in 1908. Second, to vouch that if he, Couceiro, had restored it in Porto, in 1919, it had only been in an opportunistic move.]

Within the political strategy, the question of the use of force was addressed by the creation of a civil militia, the Corpo de Voluntários da Acção Realista (VAR), which however made little progress. In outline it was similar to the *Fédération Nationale des Camelots du Roi*, created by Maurice Pujo, in 1908, and linked to Charles Maurras's *Action Française*, and its basic objective was to unite the former monarchist fighters from the incursions of 1911 and 1912 and the 'Monarchy of the North' of 1919 with a new generation of counter-revolutionaries. Its Central Command was formed of the monarchist combatants António Eça de Queiroz (son of the novelist), Álvaro dos Reis Torgal, the Conde de Calhariz, António Calainho de Azevedo, Gastão de Matos and Delfim Maia. Its Estatuto Provisório, drawn up by Luís Chaves, would be published in the journal *Acção Realista* on 15 April 1925, just three days short of the failed uprising of 18 April, led by the Frigate Captain Filomeno da Câmara, Lieutenant-Colonel of Engineers Raul Esteves and the Infantry Captain Jaime Baptista.

In the Estatuto Provisório, the Corpo de Voluntários was identified as an 'organismo de acção' [organization for action] (article no. 1), with four principal aims (no. 2): to spread the doctrines of Acção Realista Portuguesa; to set up a courier service (a network of communications between the central, district and municipal bodies and security for its propaganda activities); to organize information services for the good running of the organization; and to prepare efficient means for armed action. The priority in recruitment was for the organization of volunteers in the municipalities, and amongst the criteria for admission were 'garantia de decisão, energia, robustez' [warranty of decisiveness, energy and hardiness] (no. 6, § 3), while giving 'preferência aos combatentes da Monarquia, e depois a antigos militares ou civis não combatentes, perseguidos pela República' [preference to former combatants for the Monarchy, and then to former soldiers or non-combatant civilians persecuted by the Republic] (no. 6 § 4).

The ideological principles of Acção Realista Portuguesa were rooted in the ideas of Integralismo Lusitano,[27] which were summarized in a programme that

---

[27] Manuel Braga da Cruz, 'O integralismo lusitano nas origens do salazarismo', *Análise Social*, 70 (1982), 137–82; Paulo Archer de Carvalho, *Nação e Nacionalismo: mitemas do Integralismo Lusitano* (Coimbra: Faculdade de Letras da Universidade de Coimbra, 1993); Norberto Ferreira da Cunha, 'O Tradicionalismo Integralista', in *Poiética do Mundo: homenagem a Joaquim Cerqueira Gonçalves* (Lisbon: Colibri/Departamento de Filosofia e Centro de Filosofia da Faculdade de Letras da Universidade de Lisboa, 2001), pp. 375–99; José Manuel Quintas, *Filhos de Ramires: as origens do Integralismo Lusitano* (Lisbon: Nova Ática, 2004); Ana Isabel Sardinha Desvignes, *António Sardinha (1887–1925): um intelectual no século* (Lisbon: Imprensa de Ciências Sociais, 2006).

appeared on the back cover of every issue of *Acção Realista*:

> A organização da sociedade tendo por células primárias a *Família*, o *Município* e o *Sindicato Profissional*; A constituição dumas *Cortes Gerais* representativas dos interesses da *Igreja*, da *Terra*, da *Inteligência* e da *Produção*; Um *Rei* que *Governe* e escolha *Livremente* os seus ministros, *Responsáveis Perante Ele*; Uma *Monarquia*, enfim, liberta de todas as mentiras democráticas, expressão fiel da *Tradição Portuguesa* e do verdadeiro *Interesse Nacional*.

> [The organization of society having as its primary units the *Family*, the *Municipality*, and the *Professional Syndicate*; The constitution of the *Estates General* representative of the interests of the *Church*, of the *Land*, of *Intellectuals*, and of *Production*; A *King* who *Governs* and chooses *Freely* his ministers, *Answerable To Him*; A *Monarchy*, in short, free of all democratic deceits, a faithful expression of *Portuguese Tradition* and of the true *National Interest*.]

The ideological topoi of Acção Realista Portuguesa were the traditional monarchy (dynastic power representative of national life and with political responsibility for governance), integralist nationalism (Portuguese tradition), and organic corporativism (sociological and political). It should be noted that there was now a change in relation to the Acção Tradicionalista Portuguesa, in that there was no further reference to political parties.

Alfredo Pimenta would enter into a polemic with Catholics, both clerical and lay,[28] criticizing the official line of the Portuguese Episcopate, adopted also in the political sphere by the Centro Católico Português, of a policy of *ralliement* with the Portuguese First Republic. He believed that Catholics could not accept the Republic, for ten main reasons:

> 1) A República portuguesa é obra da Maçonaria, e a Igreja condena a Maçonaria; 2) A República portuguesa baseia-se na soberania popular, e a Igreja condena a soberania popular; 3) A República portuguesa é constitucionalmente laica, e a Igreja condena o laicismo; 4) A República portuguesa estabeleceu a Separação, na sua forma mais extrema, e a Igreja condena o princípio da Separação; 5) A República portuguesa laicizou a Família e decretou o Divórcio, e a Igreja condena a Família laica e o Divórcio; 6) A República portuguesa estabeleceu o ensino escolar laico, e a Igreja condena o ensino escolar laico; 7) A República portuguesa é racionalista, e a Igreja condena o racionalismo; 8) A República portuguesa é liberalista, e a Igreja condena o Liberalismo; 9) A República portuguesa é democrática, e a Igreja condena a Democracia política; 10) A República portuguesa é inimiga de Deus, e a Igreja é filha de Deus.[29]

---

[28] Alfredo Pimenta, *A República Portuguesa em face da Igreja Católica e a Política do Centro Católico* (Lisbon: Acção Realista Portuguesa, 1925); idem, *A Política do Centro Católico e a minha resposta ao Senhor Bispo de Bragança e Miranda* (Lisbon: Acção Realista Portuguesa, 1925).
[29] Pimenta, *A República Portuguesa em face da Igreja Católica e a Política do Centro Católico*, pp. 69–70.

[1) The Portuguese Republic is the work of the Freemasonry, and the Church condemns Freemasonry; 2) The Portuguese Republic is based on popular sovereignty, and the Church condemns popular sovereignty; 3) The Portuguese Republic is constitutionally secular, and the Church condemns secularism; 4) The Portuguese Republic has established the Separation [of Church and State], in its most extreme form, and the Church condemns the principle of Separation; 5) The Portuguese Republic has secularized the Family and decreed [in favour of] Divorce, and the Church condemns the secular Family and Divorce; 6) The Portuguese Republic has established secular school teaching, and the Church condemns secular school teaching; 7) The Portuguese Republic is rationalist, and the Church condemns rationalism; 8) The Portuguese Republic is liberalist, and the Church condemns Liberalism; 9) The Portuguese Republic is democratic, and the Church condemns political Democracy; 10) The Portuguese Republic is the enemy of God, and the Church is the daughter of God.]

Even so, it admitted that the Catholic Church had proclaimed a policy of impartiality about the different systems of government, but warned that 'uma coisa é a Igreja, como Igreja, os católicos, como católicos, e outra coisa, é os católicos, como cidadãos do Estado' [the Church as Church, the Catholics as Catholics, is one thing, Catholics as citizens of the State is another thing].[30]

The total rejection of liberal monarchy, whose political structure was based primarily on electoral suffrage (a political citizenship mediated by parties) set the doctrinal fathers of the Acção Realista Portuguesa — Alfredo Pimenta, António Cabral, Luís Chaves, Ceatano Beirão, Fernando Campos and João Ameal — on the path of a historical and ideological reinvention of the Portuguese monarchy prior to the liberal revolution of 24 August 1820, since they regarded it, from that date on, as having prepared the ground for the republican regime:

> Não se proclamam filhos da Revolução francesa, os Lenines da Rússia? Não dizem, os republicanos portugueses que, se não fosse a Monarquia liberal, nunca a República se instalaria entre nós? Não celebraram, eles, há tempos, pública e oficialmente, o Centenário da Revolução de 1820?[31]

> [Do the Lenins of Russia not proclaim themselves the children of the French Revolution? Do the Portuguese republicans not say that, were it not for the liberal Monarchy, the Republic would never have been installed here? Did they not celebrate, a while ago, publicly and officially, the Centenary of the Revolution of 1820?]

The counter-revolutionary political culture of Acção Realista Portuguesa, based on the 'trindade suprema — Deus, Pátria, Rei' [supreme trinity — God, Fatherland, King], was indebted to the counter-revolutionary political culture developed in Portugal at the end of the eighteenth century. Itself strongly influenced by the counter-revolutionary political culture in France, it made significant doctrinal acquisitions from the period of contesting the democratic

---

[30]   Pimenta, *A República Portuguesa em face da Igreja Católica e a Política do Centro Católico*, p. 65.
[31]   *Da Mensagem de 8 de Dezembro à Acção Realista Portuguesa*, p. 4.

liberalism of the Portuguese First Republic and from the new situation in Europe flowing from the First World War, which had accentuated the crisis of the liberal state in southern and central Europe. During a session in memory of the late King, D. Carlos, and the Crown Prince, D. Luís, held on 1 February 1926, Alfredo Pimenta announced an initiative for the 'geração do Resgate nacional' [generation of national Redemption]:

> Foi a minha geração quem lançou as bases do Nacionalismo integral da Nação portuguesa, ligando-se, por cima do hiato liberalista e revolucionário do século XIX, ao espírito tradicionalista que o estrangeirismo abafou em fins do século XVIII. É a minha geração quem desperta o sentimento da Catolicidade e da Realeza, e sujeita à crítica mais fria e justa o Romantismo político, laico — desnacionalizador. É da minha geração que parte o grito de alarme, e é ela que traça os delineamentos da Pátria futura.[32]

> [It was my generation that laid the foundations of the Portuguese Nation's integralist Nationalism, by linking itself, passing over the liberalist and revolutionary hiatus of the nineteenth century, to the traditionalist spirit that foreign influences smothered at the end of the eighteenth century. It is my generation that awakens the sentiment of Catholicism and Royalty, and that subjects Romanticism, political, secular — and denationalizing — to dispassionate and fair criticism. It is from my generation that the cry of alarm rises, and it is it that traces the outline of the future Fatherland.]

Pimenta recalled the importance of the idea of a 'Monarquia bem monárquica' [properly monarchical Monarchy], in which the 'Rei seja o Rei' [King should be King], and that 'acima do Rei não haja um poder dum papel' [above the King there should not be the authority of a piece of paper] (an allusion to the Constitution), advancing the idea of a 'Monarquia com o Rei livre' [Monarchy with a free King].

Fernando Campos, a member of the Administrative Committee of Acção Realista Portuguesa, wrote a work to explain the genealogy of counter-revolutionary thought in Portugal, in order to give historical legitimation to the group's social and political ideas. He published various studies in journals sympathetic to the group, and brought them together, repeatedly revised, to make a number of books.[33] He took his inspiration from a book by Louis Dimier, a member of *Action Française*, called *Les Maîtres de la Contre-Révolution au dix-neuvième siècle* (1917), and also from works by two other counter-revolutionary thinkers which had a great ideological impact in Portugal, Léon Daudet's *Le Stupide XIXe Siècle: exposé des insanités meurtrières qui se sont abattues sur la France depuis 130 ans, 1789–1919* (1922) and Georges Valois's *D'Un Siècle à l'Autre: chronique d'une génération, 1888–1920* (1924).

---

[32] Alfredo Pimenta, 'O depoimento duma geração', *Acção Realista*, February 1926, p. 36.
[33] Fernando Campos, *Os nossos mestres ou breviário da contra-revolução: juízos e depoimentos* (Lisbon: Portugália, 1924); idem, *A genealogia do pensamento nacionalista* (Lisbon: José Fernandes Júnior, 1931); idem, *O pensamento contra-revolucionário em Portugal (século XIX)*, 2 vols (Lisbon: José Fernandes Júnior, 1931–33).

For his essential selection of nineteenth-century Portuguese authors, those whom he regarded as the makers of counter-revolutionary thought in Portugal — in the fields of religion, nationalism, tradition, monarchy, the kings, the family and economic matters — Fernando Campos chose as significant examples the Marquês de Penalva, José Agostinho de Macedo, D. Francisco Alexandre Lobo (Bishop of Viseu), José Acúrcio das Neves, Joaquim de Santo Agostinho Brito França Galvão, Frei Fortunato de São Boaventura, the Visconde de Santarém, José da Gama e Castro, António Ribeiro Saraiva, D. António de Almeida, António Joaquim de Gouveia Pinto and Faustino José da Madre de Deus.

João Ameal, a leading member of Acção Realista Portuguesa, would recall the importance of later authors, from the early twentieth century, in paving the way for the 'regresso da nova geração aos caminhos nobres do Nacionalismo e do Espiritualismo católico' [return of the new generation to the noble paths of Nationalism and Catholic Spirituality], namely Carlos Malheiro Dias and Antero de Figueiredo, 'mestres de penitência' [masters of penitence], and Manuel da Silva Gaio, Eugénio de Castro, Afonso Lopes Vieira, António Correia de Oliveira and António Sardinha, 'mestres de exaltação' [masters of exultation].[34] Between 1925 and 1928 he engaged in an intense political debate in the pages of the *Jornal de Notícias*, in Porto, over the definition of the principles of Order, the conditions for its establishment, and its precursory manifestations in 1918, with the República Nova of Sidónio Pais.[35]

In this way Fernando Campos and João Ameal were looking for legitimating doctrinal sources for a new 'espírito heróico' [heroic spirit], that could mobilize the 'geração de sacrifício e de expiação' [generation of sacrifice and atonement], as Alfredo Pimenta put it, or the 'geração nova' [new generation], as João Ameal called it. Works by the authors they evoked, and by leaders of the Acção Realista Portuguesa, formed part of the list of recommended reading, alongside others who also criticized aspects of the liberal monarchy, such as Herculano, Oliveira Martins, Ramalho Ortigão and Silva Cordeiro. Some books by Alfredo Pimenta, António Cabral, Luís Costa, the Visconde do Porto da Cruz, João Ameal, Fernando Campos and Luís Chaves were the subjects of notes for readers appearing in the journal *Acção Realista*.

These counter-revolutionary political ideas of the integralist nationalists combined philosophical elements from Thomism (the centrality of Catholicism and society as a natural and organic structure), positivism (sociocracy) and vitalism (the revolt of the conscience and the desire for change), combined to form a theory of order (moral and spiritual order, unity with personal power, functional hierarchy of competences, social harmony), which was presented with a view to a radical surpassing of the Enlightenment legacy, and the legacy of the

---

[34] João Ameal, *As directrizes da nova geração* (Lisbon: Lúmen, 1925); idem, *Panorama do nacionalismo português* (Lisbon: José Fernandes Júnior, 1932).
[35] João Ameal, *A contra-revolução* (Coimbra: Atlântida, 1928).

European liberal revolutions. While not being a political or ideological element of doctrine of either Integralismo Lusitano or of Acção Realista Portuguesa, anti-Semitism and the 'Jewish peril' appeared in a significant way in António Sardinha,[36] the most accomplished thinker of Integralismo Lusitano, and also in Alfredo de Freitas Branco (Visconde do Porto da Cruz),[37] an activist on the island of Madeira, very involved in Acção Realista Portuguesa.

Between late 1925 and late 1926, Luís de Magalhães, a leading liberal monarchist, engaged in an ideological polemic with Caetano Beirão, a member of Acção Realista Portuguesa, over the definition of traditionalism, which the integralists appropriated for themselves, and counterposed to liberalism.[38] He assembled his case using a reading of the Portuguese historical and political tradition, with a view to refuting their ideological appropriation. He insisted, as a point of departure, that traditionalism (representative monarchy, national sovereignty, limited royal power) could not be confused with the politically degenerate form known as absolutism (autocratic monarchy, divine sovereignty, absolute royal power), the regime that would be broken by the liberal revolution of 1820, restored during the reign of D. Miguel, and definitively defeated with the liberal victory of 1834.

According to Luís de Magalhães, various types of traditionalism could be found in the history of the European monarchy: 'O nosso tradicionalismo é, assim, liberal, como é liberal também o tradicionalismo inglês, como era autocrático o tradicionalismo russo, como é republicano o tradicionalismo suíço, como era imperialista o tradicionalismo germânico, etc.' [our traditionalism is, thus, liberal, as English traditionalism is also liberal, just as Russian traditionalism was autocratic, as Swiss traditionalism is republican, as Germanic traditionalism was imperialist, etc.].[39] He defended the idea that the restoration and updating of Portuguese traditionalism had taken shape in the *Carta Constitucional* of 1826, by which the personal power of the King (who had granted the *Carta*) was mitigated by national representation, as expressed by two Chambers, one hereditary and nominated by the King (the Peers) — a reflection of the power of two ancient social orders (the clergy and the nobility) — and the other elected and derived from national sovereignty (the Chamber of Deputies) — a reflection of the power of the third social order (the people).

If, on the one hand, this represented a modern reconstruction of the ancient orders of the Estates General — 'a Carta respeita e mantém a velha organização social das classes, como elas se faziam representar nos Estados Gerais: clero, nobreza e povo' [the Charter respects and maintains the old social organization by classes, as they were represented in in the Estates General:

---

[36] João Medina, 'António Sardinha, anti-semita', *Cidade*, 2 (1988), 45–122.
[37] Emanuel Janes, *Nacionalismo e nacionalistas na Madeira nos anos trinta (1928–1936)*, pp. 147–75.
[38] Luís Loia, *Liberalismo constitucional, 1826–1926: o pensamento político de Luís de Magalhães* (Lisbon: Tribuna da História, 2008).
[39] Luís de Magalhães, *Tradicionalismo e constitucionalismo: estudos de história e política nacional* (Porto: Chardron, Lello & Irmão, 1927), p. 42.

clergy, nobility and people] — the risk of parliamentarism had been attenuated, in the constitutional text of 1826, by the introduction of the moderating power, attributed to the King.[40] Caetano Beirão's ideological position was opposed to individualism and liberalism, with an inclination towards 'mono-archy', which obviously distanced him from the liberal leanings of Luís de Magalhães, in this instance by contesting his theory of an articulation between traditionalism and constitutionalism, based on historical experience in Portugal.

The relationship between Acção Realista Portuguesa and the royal lieutenant Aires de Ornelas and the leaders of Causa Monárquica was always stormy. At the time of the entry of the spokesmen António Cabral, Alfredo Pimenta and José Pedro Folque to the Conselho Superior Político of Causa Monárquica, Acção Realista Portuguesa was able to safeguard its ideological and organizational independence, as was confirmed in the official note dated 31 October 1925.[41] However, D. Manuel's *Mensagem* to the monarchists in February 1926 would accentuate the divisions between the liberal and anti-liberal currents, and would have been welcomed by the political elite of Acção Realista Portuguesa, given that the King, now exiled in England, had distanced himself from the constitutional monarchy which had ended with his own overthrow on 5 October 1910. The official organ of Causa Monárquica, the daily *Correio da Manhã*, only released certain excerpts from the text, and the integralist nationalists reacted by demanding its full publication. Acção Realista Portuguesa accompanied their demand by a long Message, addressed to D. Manuel II, dated 3 April 1926 and signed by the main national and regional leaders. The representatives of Acção Realista Portuguesa had walked out of the Conselho Superior Político of Causa Monárquica on 27 March 1926, and later resigned their positions.[42] This formalized the definitive break between the two monarchists currents.

Final Considerations

Acção Realista Portuguesa ceased to exist around the end of 1926 or the beginning of 1927, in the midst of the ultimately unsuccessful reorganization of the various small groups of integralist monarchists into the Liga de Acção Integralista, being promoted by António Rodrigues Cavalheiro. An important element of this project was the launching in Lisbon, in March 1927, of a weekly paper called *A Ideia Nacional*, edited by João do Amaral (who had returned to Portugal), in collaboration with (amongst others) Alfredo Pimenta, Caetano Beirão, Fernando Campos, João Ameal, D. Luís Vieira de Castro, Armando da Silva, Armando Boaventura, Augusto da Costa, Manuel Múrias, Pedro Teotónio Pereira, Marcelo Caetano and António Rodrigues Cavalheiro. The four last-mentioned, referred to as contributors to *A Ideia Nacional*, belonged

[40]   Magalhães, *Tradicionalismo e constitucionalismo*, pp. 18–24.
[41]   *Acção Realista*, 15 December 1925, pp. 253–54.
[42]   *Acção Realista*, October 1926, pp. 97–106.

at that time to the Direcção of the Instituto António Sardinha, chaired by
Domingos de Gusmão Araújo. Between March 1926 and February 1927, Marcelo
Caetano had been the founding editor, in partnership with Albano Pereira
Dias de Magalhães, of the integralist publication *Ordem Nova*, which had this
paradoxical strapline:

> Revista anti-moderna, anti-liberal, anti-democrática, anti-burguesa e anti-
> bolchevista. Contra-revolucionária; reaccionária; católica, apostólica e
> romana; monárquica; intolerante e intransigente; insolidária com escritores,
> jornalistas e quaisquer profissionais das letras, das artes e da imprensa.
>
> [An anti-modern, anti-liberal, anti-democratic, anti-bourgeois and anti-
> bolshevik journal. Counter-revolutionary; reactionary; Catholic, apostolic
> and roman; monarchical; intolerant and intransigent; unsympathetic to
> writers, journalists and any professionals of letters, the arts and the press.]

Despite the permanent suspension of *A Ideia Nacional*, in August 1927, following
the failed revolutionary uprising of 12 August led by Filomeno da Câmara and
Fidelino de Figueiredo — the so-called conspiracy of the Fifis — its propaganda
activity, as well as being informative about the resurgence of the integralist
nationalists, is fundamental for an understanding the activities of the political
and military groups of the radical right, which under the leadership of the naval
office Filomeno da Câmara did not abandon the increasingly implausible path
of political revolution backed by military *caudilhism* and civil mobilization.

A segment of the elite of Acção Realista Portuguesa entered the political
and cultural elite of the Salazarist Estado Novo, notably Alfredo Pimenta,
Caetano Beirão, João Ameal, António Rodrigues Cavalheiro (all as historians;
João Ameal also entered the Secretariado da Propaganda Nacional (SPN)
and the Legião Portuguesa, and was the author of the *Decálogo do Estado
Novo*), Ernesto Gonçalves (as a corporative leader in Madeira), António Eça
de Queiroz (SPN), Fernando Campos (SPN, and producer of summaries of
nationalist thinking), João Pinto da Costa Leite (in the Legião Portuguesa and
in the governing elite), Bento Caldas (in the corporative elite, in Leiria) and Luís
da Câmara Pina (in the military and parliamentary elite); the last three had also
belonged to the Acção Realista Portuguesa's Direcção da Junta Escolar of the
University of Coimbra.

As has been emphasized throughout this article, the essential features of
the anti-liberal political culture that the Acção Realista Portuguesa set down
as their doctrinal heritage, based philosophically on Thomism, positivism
and vitalism, were a Catholic nationalism of an anti-Enlightenment and anti-
liberal kind, an anti-individualist and organic monarchism, an anti-democratic
political authoritarianism, a social corporativism, a professional syndicalism,
and administrative decentralization (to the level of provinces and town and city
councils). The political and ideological programme of Integralist Nationalism
articulated a discourse on the Nation, both in its objective foundations (territory
and people; *blood and soil*) and in its subjective basis (provincial identities and

national conscience; *historical memory and soul*), drawn from a number of historical, literary and ethnographic nationalist cultures.[43] Its discourse on the state (as the political and administrative organization of the Nation) was based on the urgent need, at the time, to 'invent' Portugal, to restore political authority and establish a new social consensus, the absence of which had led to a crisis of the national destiny, to the problem of public order (with a climate of latent civil war) and the instability of the political institutions, with a functional disarticulation between the legislative, executive and judicial authorities.[44]

Translated from Portuguese by Richard Correll

[43] João Leal, *Etnografias portuguesas (1870–1970): cultura popular e identidade nacional* (Lisbon: Publicações Dom Quixote, 2000); Luís Trindade, *O estranho caso do nacionalismo português: o salazarismo entre a literatura e a política* (Lisbon: Imprensa de Ciências Sociais, 2008); José Manuel Sobral, *Portugal, portugueses: uma identidade nacional* (Lisbon: Fundação Francisco Manuel dos Santos, 2012); Fernando Catroga, *A geografia dos afectos pátrios* (Coimbra: Almedina, 2013).

[44] Rui Ramos, *A segunda fundação (1890–1926)*, in José Mattoso (dir.), *História de Portugal*, vol. VI (Lisbon: Círculo de Leitores, 1994), pp. 565–665; Rui Ramos (coord.), Bernardo Vasconcelos e Sousa and Nuno Gonçalo Monteiro, *História de Portugal* (Lisbon: A Esfera dos Livros, 2009), pp. 605–25.

The Integralism of Plínio Salgado: Luso-Brazilian Relations

Leandro Pereira Gonçalves

Pontifícia Universidade Católica do Rio Grande do Sul

Ação Integralisa Brasileira [Brazilian Integralist Action] (AIB) was officially established on 7 October 1932, in São Paulo, as a political group whose purpose was to create a great national movement.[1] From that time onwards, the movement grew strongly and continued until the establishment of the Estado Novo [New State], in November 1937. It marks a rare but significant example of the existence of fascism beyond the European continent,[2] and has been regarded as the 'mais bem sucedido dos movimentos fascistas latino-americanos' [most successful of the fascist movements in Latin America].[3]

Plínio Salgado became well known as the leader of the group, which presented itself as a political movement that intended to awaken the nation. Integralism, with its forceful discourse and solid Christian basis, directed the anxieties and fears of the middle classes towards political action, making it an instrument of its incorporation into the political process. There is no doubt that integralism and Plínio Salgado reached the peak of their influence in Brazilian politics during the period of the AIB's legality, in the context of 1930s fascism as experienced in Brazil.[4] Through the movement, Plínio Salgado became strengthened as an intellectual leader with ambitious intentions in the Brazilian society of the inter-war period. In the academic studies of the integralist movement and its political thought, there is an almost exclusive concentration on the period concerned, one of the reasons for which is the importance that the AIB attained in the 1930s, especially in political relations and external influence.

The first studies on the theme were in the field of the social sciences, and are still today key points of reference for any researcher on the topic. Undoubtedly, the starting point is political scientist Hélgio Trindade's thesis, researched from

[1]   Research for this article was supported by the Fundação Calouste Gulbenkian (Portugal) and Coordenação de Aperfeiçoamento de Pessoal de Nível Superior (Brazil).
[2]   Roger Griffin, 'The Nation Reborn: A New Ideal Type of Generic Fascism', paper presented at the XV World Congress of IPSA, Buenos Aires, July 1991, pp. 33–38.
[3]   António Costa Pinto, *Os Camisas Azuis: ideologia, elites e movimentos fascistas em Portugal, 1914–1945* (Lisbon: Editorial Estampa, 1994), p. 143.
[4]   Eliana Regina de Freitas Dutra, *O ardil totalitário: imaginário político no Brasil dos anos 30* (Belo Horizonte: UFMG; Rio de Janeiro: UFRJ, 1997), p. 16.

Portuguese Studies vol. 30 no. 1 (2014), 67–93

1967 to 1971 at the Université Paris 1 (Panthéon-Sorbonne) and entitled *L'Action intégraliste brésilienne: un mouvement de type fasciste au Brésil*, translated and published in Brazil in 1974 under the title *Integralismo: o fascismo brasileiro na década de 30*. This study prompted the topic's entry into the academic milieu, making the movement better known and the object of new interpretations. Following this came a critical intervention from new research into integralism in the social sciences, the first of which was the classic 1977 doctoral thesis by José Chasin, *O Integralismo de Plínio Salgado: forma de regressividade no capitalismo hiper-tardio*, published as a monograph in 1978. Provoking much debate between its author and Trindade, this aimed to analyse Plínio Salgado's thought within a Lukacsian dialectical framework. Completed in the same year, at the University of São Paulo, Gilberto Felisberto Vasconcellos's doctoral thesis *Ideologia curupira: análise do discurso integralista* (published in 1979) introduced a third approach to the analysis of integralist thought, relating it to the modernist movement, of which the AIB leader Plínio Salgado was a member. Closing the cycle of research on integralism in the 1970s came the work of the philosopher Marilena Chauí, in her essay 'Apontamentos para uma crítica da Ação Integralista Brasileira' included in the volume *Ideologia e mobilização popular* (1978). Here, Chauí continued to work on new interpretive models of integralism based on Marxism, with a focus on the class character of the movement. This quartet (Trindade, Chasin, Vasconcellos and Chauí) has become an essential point of reference for the study of the integralist movement within the social sciences and philosophy, but only in the mid 1980s did integralism come to be analysed tentatively within the field of political history, probably as a consequence of the influence of Marxist thought and the Annales school up to this time.[5]

The AIB was founded in the wake of the debates instigated by the presence in 1920s São Paulo of Salgado, whose thinking emerged under the reformist aegis of the modernist movement. It is understood that Salgado's thinking had, at a certain moment, a crystallizing effect on the intellectual atmosphere of São Paulo, where it appeared on the agenda of the Verde-Amarelo group and of its successor, Anta:

> Das escaramuças de rua para a conversão, em 1932, na Ação Integralista Brasileira, e daí para o primeiro desfile dos 'camisas-verdes' em 23 de abril de 1933, a trajetória da 'brasilidade integral' viria marcar o último passo da aventura revolucionária do grupo. Em um de seus últimos manifestos importantes, uma reunião de textos programáticos publicada por Plínio Salgado em 1935, será possível vislumbrar [...] a proposta de reformular as

[5] Hélgio Trindade, *Integralismo: o fascismo brasileiro da década de 30*, 2nd edn (Porto Alegre: Difel/UFRGS, 1979); José Chasin, *O integralismo de Plínio Salgado: forma de regressividade no capitalismo hiper-tardio*, 2nd edn (Belo Horizonte: Una, 1999); Gilberto Felisberto Vasconcellos, *Ideologia curupira: análise do discurso integralista* (São Paulo: Brasiliense, 1979); Marilena Chauí, 'Apontamentos para uma crítica da Ação Integralista Brasileira', in *Ideologia e mobilização popular*, ed. by Maria Sylvia Carvalho Franco (São Paulo: Paz e Terra, 1985).

bases da vida cultural e institucional da Nação, visando, de um lado, superar a nossa independência intelectual e política dos centros europeus.[6]

[From street skirmishes to its conversion, in 1932, into Brazilian Integralist Action, and thence to the first parade of the 'green-shirts' on 23 April 1933, the path followed by the 'integral Brazilianness' would mark the last stage in the revolutionary adventure of the group. In one of his last important manifestos, a compilation of programmatic texts published by Plínio Salgado in 1935, it is possible to discern [...] the proposal to reformulate the underpinnings of the nation's institutional and cultural life in order to overcome our intellectual and political independence from European centres.]

Plínio Salgado's literary activities have an important bearing on the movement's political contextualization, with his novel *O estrangeiro*,[7] and his modernist activities as key elements for understanding how the AIB was conceived, since its nationalism and patriotism, the commitment to reinvent the latent 'feeling' of Brazilianness, as well as a radical conservatism, were elements common to both.[8]

The 'integral Brazilianness' proposed by Plínio Salgado for integralism had the very clear and explicit objective of synthesizing the elements taken on in the cultural and political arenas in recent years in São Paulo, with religion as a central element of discourse and action for the movement. It was at that moment, on the eve of the founding of the AIB and following the Modern Art Week, at the peak of discussions and debates about the concept of nationalism, that he identified in himself 'a passagem do *poeta-construtor* para o *homem-índice*, ou, em outros termos, do *gênio literário* para o *gênio-político*' [the transition from the *poet-builder* to the *man-index*, or, in other words, from the *literary-genius* to the *political-genius*].[9] Such expressions were used by the integralist leader without affected modesty, analysing the need for the emergence of new public men in Brazil:

> Ao Brasil tem faltado essa *virtú* nos seus homens públicos. E tem faltado, não por ausência de capacidade política, mas em consequência de não se haver ainda conjugado num único homem o alto senso teórico e o exato senso pratico, a ciência e a arte, a inteligência e a ação, a cultura e a experiência. Entretanto, nós possuímos todos os elementos para suscitar o aparecimento do nosso gênio político. Ele só poderá surgir de um movimento nacional. Sem criar o movimento em todas as províncias, não temos o direito de esperar 'um homem' [...] Nunca teremos o nosso gênio político, o nosso homem índice, se nos pusermos a sonhar e esperar aquilo que só poderá sair de nós mesmos, num Porvir que dependerá do Presente.[10]

[6] Antônio Arnoni Prado, *1922 — itinerário de uma falsa vanguarda: os dissidentes, a semana e o integralismo* (São Paulo: Brasiliense, 1983), pp. 93–94.
[7] Novel written in 1926. Plínio Salgado, *O extrangeiro*, 3rd edn (Rio de Janeiro: José Olímpio, 1936).
[8] Prado, p. 77.
[9] Prado, p. 99.
[10] Plínio Salgado, 'A "Virtú" de Machiavel', in Plínio Salgado, *Despertemos a Nação!* (Rio de Janeiro:

[Brazil has been lacking in this *virtú* in its public men. And it has been lacking, not due to a lack of political capacity, but as a result of there not yet having combined into a single man high theoretical sense and exact practical sense, science and art, intelligence and action, culture and experience. However, we have all the elements to engender the emergence of our own political genius. It can only emerge from a national movement. Without creating the movement in all the provinces, we will not have the right to expect 'a man' [...] We will never have our political genius, our index man, if we only dream and wait for what can only emerge from ourselves, in a Future that depends on the Present.]

What is worth noting here is the connection made by the author, in an article written in 1931 on the eve of the founding of the AIB, in stating that the genius would emerge from a national movement. The scholarship on Salgado does not define him as a modernist intellectual, but rather as an opportunist who used the avant-garde movement as a kind of showcase in order to make his appearance on the Brazilian political scene. As he said: 'É preciso que nós, intelectuais, tomemos conta do Brasil. Definitivamente. Temos que romper com a medíocre tradição da política. Estamos fartos de vivermos, nós, intelectuais, à sombra dos poderosos. Queremos mandar' [We intellectuals must take charge of Brazil. Definitively. We have to break with the mediocre tradition of politics. We intellectuals are tired of living in the shadow of powerful people. We want to rule].[11]

For this purpose, it was necessary to achieve a certain intellectuality, a point which he himself made in 1933, in the preface of the book *Psicologia da Revolução*, when he wrote: 'Este livro não é um livro para o povo, mas para os que pretendem influir nos destinos do povo. Aos políticos e aos intelectuais é que me dirijo nestas páginas' [This book is not a book for the people, but for those who wish to influence the destiny of the people. It is to politicians and intellectuals that I address myself in these pages].[12] This path had already been trodden by counterparts, such as the *Action Française* and *Integralismo Lusitano* (IL), which initiated reflections about literature and established a transition to politics: 'O *Integralismo Lusitano*, à semelhança da sua congênere francesa, *Action Française*, passou de literário para a atuação e influência política e o seu nacionalismo de estético-literário tornou-se político' [*Integralismo Lusitano*, like its French counterpart, *Action Française*, passed from literary to political influence and action and its aesthetic-literary nationalism became political].[13]

By analysing the formation of Portuguese integralism, we can retrieve insights from a precursor of the movement, António Sardinha, who used the thinking of the founder of *Action Française*, Charles Maurras, in order to

José Olympio, 1935), pp. 115–16.
[11]   Correspondence from Plínio Salgado to Ribeiro Couto, 5 July 1933 (Fundação Casa de Rui Barbosa/ Arquivos Pessoais de Escritores Brasileiros — FCRB/APEB-Pop: 28177).
[12]   Plínio Salgado, *Psychologia da Revolução*, 2nd edn (Rio de Janeiro: José Olympio, 1935), p. 9.
[13]   Nuno Simão Ferreira, 'A I República e os integralistas: a visão de Alberto de Monsaraz', *Lusíada: história*, 5/6 (2009), 239–93 (p. 256).

elucidate this process of transition from a literary movement to politics:

> Como Sardinha lembrará mais tarde 'Charles Maurras disse um dia [...] *les lettres nous ont conduit à la politique [...] mais notre nationalisme commence pour être esthétique*. Ao pensar um pouco nas nossas origens literárias [...] eu reconheço que também a nós as Letras nos conduziram à política.'[14]

> [As Sardinha would later recall 'Charles Maurras said one day [...] *les lettres nous ont conduit à la politique [...] mais notre nationalisme commence pour être esthétique*. On thinking a little about our literary origins [...] I realize that the Arts also led us to politics.']

There is a point of unity amongst the radical conservative movements which promoted the influence of Plínio Salgado's thinking, because for this it was necessary to reach the intelligentsia to delineate a corporativist project. Only with the endorsement of the Brazilian intelligentsia could the movement legitimize its discourse. Thus, he acted as a vanguardist, the bearer of a revolutionary discourse; however, what was at stake was the possibility of formalizing his ideas on the Brazilian political scene. In 1933, the author launched two books simultaneously, the above-mentioned *Psicologia da Revolução* and *O que é integralismo*. In the preface of the former, the author demonstrated the need to justify his actions in an intellectual tone:

> Aos políticos e aos intelectuais é que me dirijo nestas páginas. Nossa crise maior é do pensamento. Sem que esta seja resolvida, não poderemos solucionar o problema da Nação. Evidente que esse trabalho enorme não compete apenas a mim, nem me apresento com a vaidade fútil de ensinar a tantos mestres que me habituei a ouvir e cujos livros compulso. A construção é nacional e nela deve colaborar todos os brasileiros. Este livro é um convite aos intelectuais, aos políticos para que restauremos no Brasil o primado do Espírito, da Inteligência, da Virtude; para que não nos conservemos passivos a afirmar que outro recurso não há, senão deixar correr o barco. O Homem pode interferir na marcha social. E quando a sociedade está se dissolvendo, e quando vai o país a pique de se desagregar, então essa interferência deixa de ser tão só uma possibilidade, porquanto se impõe como um dever. Dedicado à massa popular, dou a público, juntamente com este, outro volume, sob o título: *O que é integralismo*. Ali começo a fazer trabalhar uma ideia na multidão. Aqui, porém, lanço a ideia nuclear, da qual deriva a outra, afim de que este livro desperte novos apóstolos de um movimento que considero o único salvador da Pátria na hora presente.[15]

[14] António Costa Pinto, 'A formação do Integralismo Lusitano (1907–17)', *Análise Social*, 18.72–74 (1982), 1409–19 (p. 1413).
[15] Salgado, *Psicologia da Revolução*, 1st edn, pp. 9–10. In 1937, on launching the 3rd edition, the author changes the discourse used in the defence of his best-selling book: 'The constant demand for this book demonstrates that it continues to be appropriate and has attained the understanding of Brazilians. [...] The incessant demand shows me that this book became a book of the people. [...] Regarding the thesis outlined here, it is completely victorious.' According to Plínio Salgado, the book is no longer solely focused on intellectuals. Plínio Salgado, *Psychologia da Revolução*, 3rd edn (Rio de Janeiro: José Olympio, 1937), pp. 5–6.

[It is politicians and intellectuals whom I address in these pages. Our major crisis is the crisis of thought. Without solving this, we can not solve the problem of the Nation. It is evident that this huge work is not up to me alone, nor do I present myself with the futile vanity of teaching so many masters whom I have listened to so often and whose books I peruse. The construction is national and all Brazilians should collaborate in it. This book is an invitation to intellectuals, to politicians, to restore in Brazil the primacy of the Spirit, of Intelligence, of Virtue, so that we do not remain passive and claim that there is no other recourse, but to let things lie. Man can interfere in the social march. And when society is in dissolution, and when the country is on the verge of crumbling, then this interference is no longer just a possibility; it is imposed as a duty. Dedicated to the mass of the people, I make public, along with this, another volume, under the title: *O que é integralismo*. There I start to make an idea work in the crowd. Here, however, I set out the core idea, from which the other derives, so that this book will awaken new apostles of a movement that I consider the saviour of the Fatherland at the present time.]

In the 1920s he was in search of an intellectual role. For this purpose, in a book destined for the 'people', he insisted on making clear the image of an intellectual who wanted to create through his personality and, principally, through the integralist movement, saying: 'O integralismo dará um altíssimo relevo aos pensadores, filósofos, cientistas, artistas, técnicos, proclamando-os supremos guias da Nação' [Integralism will give great importance to thinkers, philosophers, scientists, artists, and technicians, proclaiming them as the supreme guides of the Nation].[16] In a letter to the poet Ribeiro Couto,[17] he analysed the two works and lamented the editorial problems, especially considering the importance of the book:

Não sei se V. viu um livrinho que o Schmidt publicou: um desastre a revisão, um relaxamento a impressão. Estou indignado. Em todo o caso, passando por cima das asneiras com que os tipógrafos escangalharam com o livro, peço-lhe que o veja. Tem um tom mais panfletário do que doutrinário, porque o outro, o das elites, é o que deverá sair, chamado *Psychologia da revolução*. É nele que estão as bases filosóficas.[18]

[I do not know if you saw a little book published by Schmidt: the proof-reading is terrible, the printing careless. I am outraged. In any case, ignoring the blunders with which the typographers ruined the book, I urge you to see it. It has a tone that is more pamphleteering than doctrinal, because the other, the one for the elites, called *Psychologia da revolução*, is the one that is going to come out. That is where the philosophical foundations lie.]

In July 1933, less than a year after the founding of the AIB, Plínio Salgado boasted of the acceptance that the movement was gaining in literate society:

[16] Plínio Salgado, *O que é o integralismo*, 4th edn (Rio de Janeiro: Schmidt, 1937), p. 136.
[17] A member of the Academia Brasileira de Letras, Ribeiro Couto was an author of literary works and had published in several newspapers, including the *Correio Paulistano* alongside Plínio Salgado.
[18] Correspondence from Plínio Salgado to Ribeiro Couto, 5 July 1933 (FCRB/APEB-Pop: 28177).

'Em S. Paulo, o movimento vai crescendo. Os intelectuais estão compreendendo o alto sentido desta campanha. A classe estudantina já se conta por muitas centenas. Os estudantes estão aproveitando as férias para fazer conferências pelo interior todo' [In São Paulo, the movement keeps growing. The intellectuals are realizing the elevated nature of this campaign. The student division already numbers many hundreds. The students are taking advantage of their holidays to give lectures throughout the province].[19]

It can be seen that he assumed an intellectual role with a dual function: on the one hand to reach the intelligentsia, in order to gain the acceptance of the movement, and on the other as pamphleteer, that is, an indoctrinator and manipulator of the illiterate class. He stated: 'Este nosso movimento deve se desdobrar em dois planos: o popular, e o cultural. Enquanto um modifica o "sentimento" da massa; o outro cria os líderes, os chefes, os que deverão conduzi-la, quando vencermos' [This movement of ours must develop on two levels: the popular and the cultural. While one changes the 'feeling' of the masses, the other creates leaders, commanders, who will have to lead them, when we win].[20] An artifice such as this, applauding the intellectual, was already known to the political and cultural sectors of society, since leaders of political movements set themselves up as intellectuals in society. This is what the Integralismo Lusitano did through Hipólito Raposo, an author who, when analysing the movement, said: 'eles não podem imaginar o que foi o nosso drama intelectual, nem compreender o desvario das nossas caminhadas, através de erros sedutores que nos afiguravam certezas dogmáticas' [they can not imagine what our intellectual drama was, nor understand the folly of our paths, through seductive errors that seemed to us dogmatic certainties].[21] Plínio Salgado, on the other hand, set himself up as the bearer of the only truly intellectual movement, a visible quest for opportunistic acceptance in political society:

> O Brasil não tem tipo filósofos nem criadores do direito. O que temos tido são divulgadores, compiladores, comentadores, hermeneutas, causídicos e rábulas. Daí o nosso charlatanismo, o nosso empirismo, o nosso unilateralismo expresso no provincianismo político e no estudo em separado de cada problema nacional, que nunca se subordina ao quadro geral dos problemas nacionais. Essa é a ordem cultural que o integralismo está criando.[22]

> [Brazil has not had philosophers or lawmakers. What we have had are disseminators, compilers, commentators, interpreters, advocates of causes and pretenders. Hence our charlatanism, our empiricism, our unilateralism expressed in political provincialism and in the separate study of

---

[19] Ibid.
[20] Ibid.
[21] Hipólito Raposo, *Dois nacionalismos: L'Action Française e o Integralismo Lusitano* (Lisbon: Ferei Torres, 1929), p. 33.
[22] Plínio Salgado, 'O problema da ordem', in *A doutrina do Sigma* (São Paulo: Revista dos Tribunais, 1935), p. 42.

each national problem, which never subordinates itself to the general
framework of national problems. This is the cultural order that integralism
is creating.]

This thought was a recurring one, but ambiguities marked the organization of
Salgado's thought. In comparison with other models and political organizations,
Salgado's proposal did not represent originality. It was nothing more than an
act of theoretical mimicry, imported from the cultural centre against which he
was struggling, Europe.[23] Assuming positions in order to legitimize originality
was a constant feature of the movements that were called nationalist. The
Integralismo Lusitano, for example, stated that it was a political organization
whose intention was to reject any foreign influence.[24] Time did not allow for
influences to be acknowledged on any discourses, however obvious they might
have been, as was apparent in the lack of originality of both the Brazilian and
Lusitanian integralist movements. When we analyse the economic perspective
of the Integralismo Lusitano, it can be stated that:

> Ora foi orientação global do IL afirmar que as premissas especulativas
> da economia podem ser infletidas em duas direções muito diferentes:
> 'economia nacionalista cristã' ou 'economia materialista'. Na primeira,
> o maior grau possível de liberdade de aquisição de bens é atingível pela
> integração nacional dos fins ditados pela lei natural. Na segunda, o
> princípio hedonista deixa de ser meramente funcional para se tornar
> princípio originador de uma sociedade de tipo liberal ou de tipo soviético.
> A contraposição destas duas economias estava de há muito feita por Le Play,
> por exemplo, ou na Doutrina Social da Igreja, pelo que *os integralistas não
> foram nem pretenderam ser originais.*[25](my italics)

> [It was the overall orientation of the Integralismo Lusitano to state that the
> speculative assumptions of economics can be inflected in two very different
> directions: 'Christian nationalist economy' or 'materialist economy'. In the
> former, the greatest possible degree of freedom for the acquisition of goods
> is attainable by the national integration of the ends dictated by natural
> law. In the second the hedonistic principle ceases to be merely functional
> to become the originating principle of a society of the liberal type or the
> Soviet type. The contraposition of these two economies had been made
> long before by Le Play, for example, or in the Social Doctrine of the Church,
> from which it can be seen that *the integralists were not original nor did they
> aspire to be.*]

Besides lacking originality, the radical conservative movements cited showed
no modern features except, in the specific case of Plínio Salgado, a formal

---

[23]   Vasconcellos, *Ideologia curupira*, p. 47.
[24]   Pinto, 'A formação do Integralismo Lusitano (1907–17)', p. 1418.
[25]   Mendo Castro Henriques, 'Perspectivas ético-económicas no Integralismo Lusitano', in *Contri-
buições para a história do pensamento económico em Portugal: comunicações apresentadas no
Seminário sobre História do Pensamento Económico em Portugal organizado em outubro de 1987 pelo
Centro de Investigação sobre Economia Portuguesa (CISEP) do Instituto Superior de Economia*, ed. by
José Luís Cardoso (Lisbon: D. Quixote, 1988), p. 153.

fragmentation full of intertextuality. The latter can be characterized as a modernist project because the content and related aspects in the political process of the author were nothing more than concepts theorized in the nineteenth century and contextualized in an anti-materialist environment, as characterized by the release of *Rerum Novarum*.[26]

With a discourse based on a set of Christian truths, the encyclical was created with the intention of achieving a society in transformation:

> A doutrina social da Igreja é um conjunto de ideias ou concepções (feitas de verdades, de princípios e de valores), que o Magistério vivo fundamenta na lei natural e na Revelação, e que adapta e aplica aos problemas sociais do nosso tempo, a fim de, segundo a maneira própria da Igreja, ajudar os povos e os governantes a organizar uma sociedade mais humana e mais conforme aos desígnios de Deus sobre o mundo.[27]

> [The Church's social doctrine is a set of ideas or conceptions (made of truths, principles and values) that the living Magisterium bases on natural law and Revelation, and which it adapts and applies to the social problems of our time, in order, according to the way of the Church, to help the people and their leaders to organize a society that is more humane and more in conformity with God's plans for the world.]

By means of the papal encyclical of Leo XIII, radical movements of a conservative nature began to organize themselves and appear worldwide in response to the doctrine. That is, there occurred a form of application of the social theory of the church, and the AIB had as one of its major theoretical foundations this need, observed in the Christian community, for the applicability of such dogmas in the twentieth century: 'Uma das influências mais fortes que o integralismo recebeu adveio, claramente, da concepção cristã do mundo' [One of the strongest influences that integralism received clearly came from the Christian conception of the world].[28] Similar elements occurred in several localities in the western world, especially the above-mentioned Integralismo Lusitano which drew its inspiration from Maurras's *Action Française*.

The thinking of Plínio Salgado was born from the influence of Integralismo Lusitano, which is derived from Maurrasianism, from the Social Doctrine of the Church, as well as some aspects of the doctrine and practice of Italian Fascism, from which regime it adopted the one-party state corporatist model. Within these conceptions, allied to nationalist-Christian auto-didacticism, as well as the influence of the family and the need for a vanguard discourse, the AIB was born. In 1891, Pope Leo XIII started a struggle against what was called the 'exploitation of the workers', but at the same time, he was in opposition to the

[26] Papal encyclical *Rerum Novarum* (1891) available online at <http://www.vatican.va/holy_father/leo_xiii/encyclicals/documents/hf_l- xiii_enc_15051891_rerum-novarum_en.html> [accessed 18 June 2011].

[27] Émile Mons Guerry, *Doutrina social da Igreja* (Lisbon: Sampedro; São Paulo: Herder, 1960), p. 9.

[28] Antônio Rago Filho, 'A crítica romântica à miséria brasileira: o integralismo de Gustavo Barroso' (unpublished masters dissertation, Pontifícia Universidade Católica de São Paulo, 1989), p. 157.

principle of class struggle and Marxism.[29] He started to see and defend religion as an element of reform and social justice, while for Marx such changes could occur only through revolution. There was an appeal in Catholic thought to the Christian spirit in order that employers would respect their workers. Thus the church reached different social sectors with the main purpose undoubtedly of keeping materialist thinking divorced from power, thereby preventing any kind of opposition to Western Christian domination.

A significant part of the opposition to Marxism was based around an anti-materialistic conservative brand of Christian thought, the central tenet of the views formulated in 1891 by Leo XIII and his encyclical, the *Rerum Novarum*, seen by the church as fundamental:

> Primera de las grandes encíclicas sociales de los tiempos modernos, la *Rerum Novarum* sigue siendo hoy [...] la *Carta Magna del Trabajo*, principio y fundamento de la enseñanza social de la Iglesia. León XIII la proyectó como el más formidable aldabonazo sobre las consciencias de los cristianos de su época, en defensa de la clase obrera. Pero sus dotes excepcionales de Maestro y Pastor la convirtieron en una de las obras cumbres de su ingente labor doctrinal, cuya luz, lejos de disminuir con el tiempo, ha ido ganando en claridad y en trascendencia práctica.[30]

> [First of the great social encyclicals of modern times, the *Rerum Novarum* remains today [...] the *Magna Carta of Labour*, the principle and foundation of the Church's social teaching. Leo XIII designed it as the most formidable and accurate theory on the consciences of Christians of his age, in defence of the working class. But the outstanding skills of the teacher and church minister transformed it into one of the supreme works of his huge doctrinal oeuvre, whose light, far from fading over time, has gained in clarity and practical transcendence.]

The Brazilian integralist leader, loyal to Catholic dogma, did not remain passive towards the words coming from the Vatican. Salgado's thinking with regard to Brazilian politics was established in this context, since elements to combat communism and liberalism were central conceptions whose purpose, in the words of Leo XIII, was to 'proclamar o cristianismo como a única forma de

---

[29] But earlier, Pope Pius IX had undertaken intense struggles against the liberalism and communism that was emerging in the mid-nineteenth century. The Pope defined the ideas of freedom coming from the bourgeois philosophers as the main form of destruction of Christian spiritual order. Pius IX began a campaign against what he called false liberalism and in the encyclical *Quanta Cura* of 1864 he condemned sixteen propositions that contradicted the Catholic vision at the time. This encyclical was accompanied by *Syllabus errorum*, which condemned conceptions like rationalism, socialism, communism, Freemasonry and Judaism. Regarding the Christian struggle he states: 'There remains no alternative to salvation in this world, nor to the Church itself, except "the conversion of sinners, the diffusion of the Catholic faith, the sanctity of the clergy, the good example of all believers", in short, the salvation of individual souls faced with corrupting liberalism, which destroyed the only possible unity, the unity of the Faith. It should be noted as well, that one of the "essential and eternal truths" that embraces integralism resides in consideration of social inequality among men as a natural and immutable condition.' Rago Filho, 'A crítica romântica à miséria brasileira', p. 177.
[30] Comisión Episcopal Apostolado Social, *Doctrina social de la iglesia: desde la 'Rerum Novarum' a la 'Mater Magistra'* (Madrid: E. Sánchez Leal, 1963), p. 16.

se criar uma justiça social, por meio de um apelo às consciências individuais, concitando-os, sem distinção de classe e de credo, ao mesmo espírito social caridoso' [proclaim Christianity as the only way to create social justice through an appeal to individual consciences, inciting them, without distinction of class and creed, to the same charitable social spirit].[31]

Integralismo Lusitano was structured under the same Catholic influence.[32] We highlight the categorical relationship between the message of the Pope and the political characterization defended by the Portuguese movement: 'Este modelo era totalmente decalcado do corporativismo ou do sindicalismo de inspiração católica no conjunto de medidas que formavam a doutrina social da Igreja, como demonstrada na encíclica *Rerum Novarum* (1891) do Papa Leão XIII' [This model was totally plagiarized from corporatism or from syndicalism of Catholic inspiration in the set of measures that formed the Church's social doctrine, as demonstrated by the encyclical *Rerum Novarum* (1891) of Pope Leo XIII].[33] When we analyse the political components that exist in the work of Alberto Monsaraz, one of the leaders of the Portuguese movement, we see that:

> Inspirou-se amplamente no pensamento da doutrina social da Igreja, preconizada pelo Papa Leão XIII na sua encíclica *Rerum Novarum* de 1891. A doutrina social da Igreja afigurava-se ao entendimento integralista como um caminho orientador da sociedade para a realização da felicidade, através da explicitação da lei natural, que era o fundamento das relações sociais.[34]

> [He was broadly inspired by the thinking of the Church's social doctrine, preached by Pope Leo XIII in his encyclical *Rerum Novarum* of 1891. The social doctrine of the Church appeared to the integralist understanding of a guiding path for society to the realization of happiness, through the explanation of natural law, which was the foundation of social relations.]

The discourse practised by the Church as a guiding path for society at the time of creation of the social doctrines took an apolitical approach as its basis, finding in God the answer to such creations. In 1981, Pope John Paul II, in *Laborem Exercens*, on human labour, argued:

> In fact the Church's social teaching finds its source in Sacred Scripture, beginning with the Book of Genesis and especially in the Gospel and the writings of the Apostles. From the beginning it was part of the Church's teaching, her concept of man and life in society, and, especially, the social morality which she worked out according to the needs of the different ages. This traditional patrimony was then inherited and developed by the

---

[31] Rago Filho, 'A crítica romântica à miséria brasileira', p. 180.
[32] Henriques, 'Perspectivas ético-económicas no Integralismo Lusitano', p. 153.
[33] Nuno Simão Ferreira, 'Alberto de Monsaraz e a vaga dos nacionalismos e dos radicalismos político-autoritários europeus do pós-I Guerra mundial: um rumo até o fascismo?', *Lusíada: história*, 4 (2007), 269–337 (p. 283).
[34] Nuno Simão Ferreira, 'A I República e os integralistas', p. 256.

teaching of the Popes on the modern 'social question', beginning with the Encyclical Rerum Novarum.[35]

In 1891, Pope Leo XIII fiercely rejected any solution that was proposed involving the socialist or liberal sectors. For him, the condition of misery in which the workers lived was an element of debate and discussion, the combat against these two tendencies being essential to the progress of a Christian social indoctrination of believers because, 'sendo a doutrina social da Igreja um corpo de princípios hauridos, em última instância, nas Sagradas Escrituras, só poderá ser vinculativa para aqueles que acreditem nas mesmas escrituras' [since the social doctrine of the Church is a body of principles drawn, ultimately, from the Holy Scriptures, it can only be binding for those who believe in those scriptures].[36]

The encyclical of 1891 can be pointed to as 'um dos grandes acontecimentos da Igreja' [one of the great achievements of the Church],[37] given the importance in the late nineteenth century of the 'social problem' in certain countries, and the rise of the working-class and socialist movements. In order to offset any action on the part of these movements, the encyclical aimed to attend ideologically to the interests of the working class and bourgeoisie (despite the pontiff's critique of liberal doctrine). Based on this discourse, several extreme conservative movements created their organizational conceptions. Beyond the above-mentioned Integralismo Lusitano, we can see in the words of Plínio Salgado ideas derived from the social doctrine of the Church. In the Manifesto of October 1932, which is the official founding document of the AIB, he said: 'A questão social deve ser resolvida pela cooperação de todos, conforme a justiça e o desejo que cada um nutre de progredir e melhorar' [The social question must be solved by the cooperation of all, in accordance with justice and the desire that each one nurtures to progress and improve].[38] In short, religious doctrine, with a nod to the social question, took on a crucial role in the course of its transition from literary creation to political action, arguing repeatedly that integralism is an 'afirmação de espiritualismo' [assertion of spirituality].[39] One can define Salgado as an intellectual who studied and sought inspiration in both Maurras and the encyclicals of Leo XIII — Rerum Novarum, particularly — to elaborate his thinking. After all, this was not a new discourse, but it did need to appear to the Brazilian intelligentsia as an original, vanguard current, hence its ambitious

---

[35] *Laborem Exercens*: To His Venerable Brothers in the Episcopate to the Priests to the Religious Families to the Sons and Daughters of the Church and all men of good will on Human Work on the ninetieth anniversary of Rerum Novarum (1981), online at <http://www.vatican.va/holy_father/john_paul_ii/encyclicals////documents/hf_jpii_enc_1409191_laborem-exercens_en.html> [accessed 18 June 2011].
[36] Augusto da Silva, 'Continuidade e inovação na doutrina social da Igreja', *Análise Social*, 123/24 (1993), 775–86 (p. 781).
[37] António José Fernandes, *Social-Democracia e Doutrina Social da Igreja: incompatíveis ou convergentes?* (Lisbon: Publicações Dom Quixote, 1979), p. 91.
[38] Plínio Salgado, *Manifesto de outubro de 1932* (Rio de Janeiro: Secretaria Nacional de Propaganda, 1932).
[39] Plínio Salgado, 'Mensagem na semana heroica', in *Cartas aos camisas verdes* (Rio de Janeiro: José Olympio, 1935), p. 131.

entrance into the modernist movement of the 1920s, which raised the status and name of the author from a simple provincial *paulista* [person from São Paulo state] to a respected intellectual in the literary and Christian nationalist political circles of São Paulo.

To understand the origins of Brazilian Integralism, especially the political thought of Plínio Salgado, we must consider, in addition to the social doctrine of the church, the origins of its European counterpart, Integralismo Lusitano. The inspiration for the Portuguese group lies in the movement conceived by Charles Maurras, *Action Française*.[40] In this regard, to understand Salgado's thinking we should analyse the French organization which, like Integralismo Lusitano, 'simultaneamente nacionalista e estrangeirado [...] recolheu, em síntese, a tradição antiliberal e católica portuguesa e o pensamento contrarrevolucionário, com uma forte matriz francesa, maurrasiana e positivista' [simultaneously nationalist and foreign-influenced [...] brought together, in a synthesis, the Portuguese Catholic and anti-liberal tradition and counter-revolutionary thought, with a strong French, Maurrasian and positivist matrix].[41] Maurrasianism is defined as the original discourse of authoritarian thought. It was in *Action Française* that revolutionary doctrines based on conservative nationalist thought searched for elements of inspiration across various political movements of the twentieth century,[42] making the study of the origins and existence of fascist movements elsewhere in Europe fundamental for an understanding of French fascism.[43]

In making the connection between the *Rerum Novarum* and *Action Française*, in the context of Plínio Salgado's thinking, this study does not intend to claim that the social doctrine of the church and the French movement were directly related; on the contrary, the policy of Leo XIII saw the monarchist thinking of Charles Maurras as its antagonist, in several senses. Despite its conservative and paternalist conception, the Church's social doctrine was not an attractive formula to *Action Française*, while in its turn the Church took on the role of condemning the French movement, despite the strong Catholic foundations of its programme: 'Basking in the glory of its Catholic credentials, *Action Française* was totally unprepared for the deluge that overwhelmed it less than a year after it had reached the zenith of its ecclesiastical prestige.'[44] Rather, we propose here to analyse this Franco-Lusitanian relationship in its theoretical aspects, together with the version practised in Italy, as elements of a Brazilian

[40]   Stewart Lloyd-Jones, 'Integralismo Lusitano: "made in France"?', *Penélope: Revista de História e Ciências Sociais*, 28 (2003), 93–106.
[41]   Ferreira, 'A I República e os integralistas', p. 256.
[42]   In the second part of the work *Integralismo e o mundo* (1936), the Head of the AIB Militias, Gustavo Barroso, developed a list of movements that were understood by him as fascist. Under the heading 'Fascism in France' he points to *Action Française* and under 'Fascism in Portugal', to Monarchist Integralism and the National Syndicalist Movement. Gustavo Barroso, *Integralismo e o mundo* (Rio de Janeiro: Civilização Brasileira, 1936).
[43]   Ernst Nolte, *Three Faces of Fascism: Action Française, Italian Fascism, National Socialism* (New York: Holt, Rinehart and Winston, 1966).
[44]   Oscar L. Arnal, *Ambivalent Alliance: The Catholic Church and the Action Française, 1899–1939* (Pittsburgh, PA: University of Pittsburgh Press, 1985), p. 123.

discourse based on Salgado's thinking:

> The relationship between the Action Française and fascism must not be regarded as one of cause and effect. Direct influences do exist, but by the same token even Italian nationalism — which of all the elements of fascism had the most contact with the Action Française — is not to be genetically deduced from it. On the other hand, they are certainly not merely parallel phenomena. If it is true that the practice of a small political group hardly bears comparison with that of a victorious mass movement in the twenty years of its unrestricted rule, it is also true that the precise, self-contained doctrine of the Action Française, and the often wavering, continually evolving doctrine of Italian fascism, do not move on the same plane.[45]

Nevertheless the fixing of doctrine was a recurrent feature of Portuguese politics and society: 'apesar da consciência dos males engendrados pela *Action Française* entre os jovens católicos' [despite an awareness of the evils engendered by *Action Française* among young Catholics],[46] doctrinal and political continuity was maintained and transported to Brazil, even after the condemnation of the movement by the Catholic Church, which accused Maurras of putting politics above religion.[47] The prohibition from the Vatican was unable to prevent the dissemination of the movement's ideas in Brazil: 'Católicos brasileiros, já familiarizados com a *Action Française* e que buscavam nela inspiração, mantiveram-se identificados com o *Integralismo Lusitano*' [Brazilian Catholics, already familiar with the *Action Française* and who sought inspiration in it, continued to identify with *Integralismo Lusitano*].[48] In fact, one of the great points of reference for Plínio Salgado was the leading Brazilian neo-Catholic Jackson de Figueiredo,[49] and the practices of the Centro Dom Vital.[50]

As regards the spread of the French conservative movement, it can be seen that 'L'influence de la doctrine de l'Action française se faisait plus fortement sentir dans les pays latins' [the influence of the doctrine of *Action Française* was felt more strongly in Latin countries],[51] even reaching Latin American countries

---

[45]   Nolte, *Three Faces of Fascism*, p. 145.
[46]   Maria Lúcia de Brito Moura, 'A condenação da *Action Française* por Pio XI: repercussões em Portugal', *Revista de História das Ideias*, 29 (2008), 545–82 (p. 558).
[47]   Teresa Malatian, *Império e missão: um novo monarquismo brasileiro* (São Paulo: Nacional, 2001), p. 85.
[48]   Ibid.
[49]   Jackson de Figueiredo (1891–1928) was a lawyer, teacher, journalist, philosopher and politician who converted to Catholicism and developed a large Catholic movement in Brazil to combat liberalism and communism. The organization established as the Centro Dom Vital is of fundamental importance for the understanding of the integralist movement in Brazil.
[50]   The Centro Dom Vital was established by Jackson de Figueiredo in 1922, with the assistance of Dom Leme. 'The definition of their role is directly linked to the Brazilian social conjuncture. [...] A spirit of excitement and renovation emerged in the post-war period. Political institutions were beginning to come into crisis. [...] The Centro Dom Vital was organized in order to catechize the laws, fighting for peace [...] finally, to contribute to the episcopate in the work of re-catechization of the intelligentsia.' Romualdo Dias, *Imagens de ordem: a doutrina católica sobre a autoridade no Brasil* (São Paulo: Unesp, 1996), pp. 89–90.
[51]   Olivier Compagnon, 'Étude comparée des cas argentin et brésilien', in *Charles Maurras et*

such as Mexico, Argentina and Brazil.[52]

> Les premiers échos du maurrassisme se font entendre dès la charnière des XIXe et XXe siècles comme en témoigne une série d'indices ponctuels. Ainsi un cercle d'Action française est-il actif à Rio de Janeiro dans la première moitié des années 1900, organisant des conférences qui font l'objet d'annonces ou de compte rendus dans la presse, mais semblent principalement destinées à la petite communauté française installée dans la capitale brésilienne.[53]

> [The first echoes of Maurrasianism are heard from the turn of the nineteenth to the twentieth century, testified by a series of proofs. Thus, a circle of *Action Française* operates in Rio de Janeiro in the first half of the 1900s, organizing conferences which result in announcements or commentaries in the press, but they seem to be targeted mainly at the small French community located in the Brazilian capital.]

In the post-war context, Maurrasianism became a privileged discourse within the Brazilian Catholic intellectual groups,[54] reflected also in the Centro Dom Vital, in Rio de Janeiro. This organization was created in 1922 on the initiative of Jackson de Figueiredo,[55] who saw in the reaffirmation of Catholicism in Brazil a spiritual necessity, after the changes of the late nineteenth century.[56]

In Jackson de Figueiredo there is greater emphasis on this understanding, particularly through the existing relations with Integralismo Lusitano and the theories of *Action Française*. At the level of theory one can perceive a relationship between Salgado and Figueiredo in their common defence of extreme nationalism of a conservative nature. Figueiredo found in Integralismo Lusitano a deepening of Maurrasian ideals, and in the eyes of some members of the Brazilian movement the connection was both doctrinal and political. In 1947, in a speech in the District Chamber in Rio de Janeiro, the integralist councillor Jayme Ferreira da Silva remarked that Jackson de Figueiredo was 'considerado com razão, como precursor do Integralismo, citando que foi Jackson, quem trouxe ao conhecimento dos brasileiros a obra de António Sardinha' [correctly regarded as the precursor of Integralism, pointing out that it was Jackson who brought the work of António Sardinha to the attention of Brazilians].[57]

In highlighting the strength of the Portuguese movement, I endorse Pinto's view 'que ele inspirou não só alguns grupos brasileiros que iriam desembocar

---

l'étranger, l'étranger et Charles Maurras: L'Action française — culture, politique, société II, ed. by Olivier Dard and Michel Grunewald (Bern: Peter Lang, 2009), p. 283.
[52]   The Lusitanian Integralists defended the operationalization of a common zone of Latin language and Latinity, consisting of the Western European nations of France, Belgium, Spain and Portugal, later to be joined by Brazil, Argentina and Mexico. Ferreira, 'Alberto de Monsaraz e a vaga dos nacionalismos', p. 295.
[53]   Compagnon, 'Étude comparée', p. 286.
[54]   Compagnon, p. 287.
[55]   Ibid.
[56]   Compagnon, pp. 287–88.
[57]   Jayme Ferreira Silva, *A verdade sobre o integralismo: discurso pronunciado na Câmara do Distrito Federal na Sessão de 9 de julho de 1947* (Rio de Janeiro: Imprensa Nacional, 1947), p. 7.

na *Ação Integralista Brasileira*, como ainda foi uma das referências da *Acción Española* (1931), com quem mantiveram estritas relações [that he not only inspired some Brazilian groups that would end up in *Ação Integralista Brasileira*, but he was also one of the references for *Acción Española* (1931), with whom he maintained close relations].[58] The condemnation of *Action Française* by the Vatican did not pose an obstacle to the growth of Brazilian integralist nationalism, and did not prevent

> [...] la fréquentation du maurrassisme par la génération brésilienne du *renacimiento católico*. En témoigne l'exemple d'Alceu Amoroso Lima, qui célébré dans un ouvrage de 1932 'le nationalisme intégral que Maurras systématisa et que Mussolini mit en pratique'. En terre lusophone, le nationalisme prit toutefois un tour radicalement différent avec la création de l'Ação Integralista Brasileira en octobre 1932, considérée par l'historiographie comme le seul véritable fascisme latino-américain. L'Action Intégraliste Brésilienne permit en effet de fédérer de nombreux pôles du nationalisme brésilien autour de la figure charismatique de Plínio Salgado [...]. En outre, Salgado et quelques outres produisirent des milliers de pages afin de jeter les bases d'une doctrine nationaliste spécifiquement brésilienne, qui ne se résumerait pas à l'importation de modèles de pensée européens ou qui, du moins, s'en émanciperait au nom même du projet politique dont est porteur le parti. Cela explique que Maurras et l'Action française soient cités occasionnellement au sein de cet abondant corpus, mais ne constituent en aucun cas les matrices de l'intégralisme ainsi qu'on a pu parfois l'écrire. Certes, l'Action Intégraliste Brésilienne identifie clairement les ennemis de la nation brésilienne en dénonçant le libéralisme, le socialisme, le capitalisme international et les sociétés secrètes liées aux Juifs et à la maçonnerie, autrement dit une variante des quatre Etats confédérés. Certes, la critique du suffrage universel et du système démocratique formulée par Salgado fait bien écho au maurrassisme.[59]

> [[...] the Brazilian generation of the Catholic renaissance from participating in Maurrasianism. This is illustrated by the example of Alceu Amoroso Lima who celebrates in a famous work of 1932 'the integral nationalism that Maurras systematized and that Mussolini put into practice'. In Lusitanian lands, nationalism took a dramatically different course, however, with the creation in October 1932 of *Ação Integralista Brasileira*, considered by historiography as the only true Latin American fascism. *Ação Integralista Brasileira* in fact made it possible to gather many poles of Brazilian nationalism around the charismatic figure of Plínio Salgado [...]. On the other hand Salgado and some others produced thousands of pages in order to lay the foundations of a particularly Brazilian nationalist doctrine that cannot be simply reduced to the importation of European models of thought, or at least that emancipate them in the name of the political project that the party defended. This explains why Maurras and *Action Française* have been cited abundantly in the corpus, but do not represent in any way the matrices of integralism as is sometimes presented. Certainly, Ação Integralista

[58]   Pinto, *Os Camisas Azuis*, p. 33.
[59]   Compagnon, 'Étude comparée', pp. 294–95.

Brasileira clearly identifies the enemies of the Brazilian nation, denouncing liberalism, socialism, international capitalism and secret societies linked to Freemasonry and the Jews, in other words a variant of the four confederate states. Indeed, the criticism of universal suffrage and the democratic system formulated by Salgado was based on Maurrasianism.]

If we analyse the thinking of the Brazilian integralist leader we will encounter some questioning of the relationship between Maurrasianism and Latin America: 'Néanmoins, on ne peut qu'être frappé par l'absence de toute référence à l'Action française dans des ouvrages aussi fondamentaux que *O que é integralismo* de Salgado' [However, we are inevitably struck by the total absence of references to *Action Française* in fundamental works like Salgado's *O que é integralismo*].[60] The pursuit of originality[61] would never allow him to surrender in the face of a doctrinal force, especially a European one: 'A constatação de um desequilíbrio entre o *país legal* e o *país real*, como diria Charles Maurras, incita o autor, ainda de uma maneira fragmentária, à crítica da *utopia democrática*' [The confirmation of an imbalance between the *legal country* and the *real country*, as Charles Maurras would say, incites the author, even in a fragmentary way, to criticize the *democratic utopia*].[62] This matter of the impossibility of democratic application is just one example of the many perspectives within *Action Française* that laid the foundations for Integralismo Lusitano and its intermediary role vis-à-vis Latin America and the AIB.

It is noted that 'Maurras, no entanto, sendo, como para muitos outros integralistas portugueses, o ponto de partida da sua formação política e intelectual, seria ultrapassado nos anos 20 por outras influências mais duradouras' [while Maurras was, as for many other Portuguese integralists, the starting point of their political and intellectual formation, he would be replaced in the 1920s by other more enduring influences].[63] That is, fascism proved a

---

[60] Compagnon, p. 295.
[61] In his 1936 work *Integralismo e o mundo*, with the aim of demonstrating the affinities between AIB and the fascist perspective, Gustavo Barroso promoted the translation of some journalistic articles about integralism in US periodicals: 'Na importante revista hispano-americana que se publica em Nova Iorque, *La Nueva Democracia*, no seu número de fevereiro de 1935, o professor Richard Pattee, reitor da Universidade de Porto Rico, publicou o seguinte artigo [...] o movimento integralista é um [...] fascismo adaptado à realidade brasileira, transplantado e modificado no solo americano, proclamando com outro nome, porém no fundo pretendendo-se às doutrinas conhecidas do Velho Mundo. [...] O mesmo crítico estampou a seguinte nota no número de abril de 1935, na revista *Books Abroad*, órgão oficial da Universidade de Oklahoma, nos Estados Unidos [...] que o integralismo é um fascismo apropriado à realidade brasileira' [In the important Hispanic-American review that is published in New York, *La Nueva Democracia*, in its last edition of February 1935, Professor Richard Pattee, Dean of the Universidade de Puerto Rico, published the following article [...] the integralist movement is a [...] fascism adapted to the Brazilian reality, modified and transplanted on American soil, proclaiming under another name, but in its core laying claim to the well-known doctrines of the Old World. [...] The same critic added the following note in the April 1935 edition of the magazine *Books Abroad*, the official organ of the University of Oklahoma in the United States, [...] that integralism is a fascism adapted to the Brazilian reality]. Barroso, *Integralismo e o mundo*, pp. 230–33.
[62] Trindade, *Integralismo*, p. 51 (my italics).
[63] Pinto, *Os Camisas Azuis*, p. 38.

much more viable and profitable relationship for the success of the AIB, as it did for part of Integralismo Lusitano, which had joined the political venture via the National-Syndicalist Movement. Also in 1922, Rolão Preto, the greatest Portuguese enthusiast, said: 'as notícias que nos vêm da Itália como as que nos chegam de França são as mais consoladoras e cheias de promessas' [the news that comes to us from Italy, like the news that comes to us from France, is the most comforting and full of promise].[64]

Paths of similarity and proximity demonstrate at all levels an intense affinity between one group and the other. Maurrasianism was the root of Salgado's thinking, alongside several other conservative elements of an extreme nature. However, within this theoretical perspective, Plínio Salgado saw a better practical foundation in the Italian Fascist movement.

It is understood that the seduction of Plínio Salgado by the fascism of Mussolini overtook his relationship to the Portuguese movement, but since the origin of both lies in the fascist elements of *Action Française*,[65] it is not possible to disarticulate so easily the analytical process, since Salgado's doctrinal development intersects at several points in these external relationships. But, as the contact between the different forms of integralism operated in the realm of ideas, I have opted to start by defining the practical terrain on which this occurred, which was the Italian movement. Later we can examine the Lusitanian and the Brazilian movements comparatively and in relation to Plínio Salgado's political and doctrinal trajectory.

In 1930, Plínio Salgado made a trip to Italy which he experienced as a transformative milestone in his thinking in the creation of a truly practical interpretation of reactionary and nationalist discourse in Brazil. He returned to Brazil full of passionate praise for fascism and with high expectations: 'A doutrina fascista estabelece o Estado, como o espelho perfeito do homem, como a própria ampliação do indivíduo' [The fascist doctrine establishes the state as the perfect mirror of man, as the very extension of the individual],[66] he said. The intention of this essay is not to intervene in the debate, under way for decades now, as to whether integralism was fascist or not, but rather to analyse the matrices of Plínio Salgado's discourse, as one self-evidently partisan to the fascist doctrine prevailing in nineteenth-century France. If, in the formation of integralism in Brazil, religious and political elements converged with nationalist discourse under the aegis of *Action Française*, Italian Fascism offered the chief practical example of how these forces could lead to and inform a movement in action.

It was on Saturday 14 June 1930, at 6pm, that Salgado managed to get an audience with the Italian leader, Benito Mussolini. For many years this

---

[64] Rolão Preto, 'A Monarquia Social', *Nação Portuguesa: revista de cultura nacionalista*, 2nd series, 6 (1922), p. 276.
[65] Nolte, *Three Faces of Fascism*.
[66] Plínio Salgado, 'Como eu vi a Itália', *Hierarchia*, March/April 1932, p. 204.

meeting was seen as full living proof of the relationship between Salgado and the Italian leader. More recent research, however,[67] reveals that it was nothing more than a brief fifteen-minute meeting,[68] a formal event devoid of any mystery. What is important, though, is that from that moment Salgado himself appeared enchanted by the practical implementation of the anti-communist and anti-liberal discourse preached by Leo XIII and the radical conservative ideas elaborated by Charles Maurras. Based on a spiritual organization of a conservative and nationalist nature, the indoctrination that he was setting up in Brazil was now becoming consolidated in the form of the AIB.

In 1932, Salgado wrote an article for the *Revista Hierarchia*, which was also republished as a pamphlet in the same year by the Sociedade Editora Latina, directed by Professor Ferruccio Rubbiani, who was one of the cultural advisors to the Italian consulate. Rather curiously, this document was not included in the official list of the author's bibliographical references, nor was it included in his *Obras Completas*, released in the 1950s. The reason, though, is clear enough. In this material Plínio Salgado developed open and explicit praise of the fascist regime and, as such, this self-image was one he wished to erase after the Second World War. Consistent with this, in none of the author's subsequent publications can we find a trace of the declarations of praise which, a month after his meeting with the Italian fascist leader, he inserted in an article published in the Rio-based newspaper *O Paiz*, calling for a similar movement in Brazil:

> Mussolini me receberia, às 18 horas. A mim e aos meus companheiros de excursão pela Itália. [...] Tudo correu para nós tão fácil e tão rápido, que fomos levados a concluir: Mussolini gosta dos intelectuais e gosta do Brasil. [...] Todo esse espetáculo da Nova Itália era a criação milagrosa de um homem, que eletriza as multidões, porque é portador de uma ideia, que arrasta, atrás de si o tropel que retumba, de uma nacionalidade que marcha, irrevogavelmente, porque leva nas suas mãos o facho aceso da inteligência. Esse o homem com quem íamos palestrar. [...] Ao avistar-nos, caminha ao nosso encontro. Nós avançamos para ele, de olhos fixos. E, nesse, instante, como a claridade de uma luz, com uma expressão de bondade infinita, acolhedora e carinhosa, ouvimos uma voz límpida, que desarma todas as minhas frases protocolares, que nos põe à vontade, felizes e tranquilos: — Sede bem-vindos amigos brasileiros! Era a voz de Mussolini. Boa e simples. É a figura do Duce, modesta e afetuosa. É o maior vulto da Europa contemporânea, e que forma, com Lenine e Gandhi, o grande tríptico da Humanidade de hoje, é ele que se faz pequeno na intimidade, ou talvez maior, porque toda grandeza é simples... [...] Mussolini é um emotivo. Observei-o a certos trechos da nossa palestra. Sinal do gênio.[69]

---

[67] The research was conducted by historian João Fábio Bertonha (UEM).
[68] Archivio Centrale dello Stato, Segretaria Particolare del Duce, Carteggio Ordinario, Udienze, b. 3102, f. giugno/1930.
[69] Plínio Salgado, 'Mussolini e o Brasil Novo', *O Paiz*, 27 July 1930.

[Mussolini would receive me at 6 pm. Myself and my travelling companions in Italy. [...] Everything went so easily and so swiftly for us, that we were led to conclude: Mussolini likes intellectuals and likes Brazil. [...] This whole spectacle of the New Italy was the miraculous creation of one man, who electrifies crowds because he is the bearer of an idea that lingers behind him in the murmuring crowd, of a nation marching irrevocably, because he holds in his hands the torch of intelligence. This is the man we were going to talk to. [...] When he saw us, he walked towards us. We went up to him, staring. And at this moment, like the brightness of a light, with an expression of infinite goodness, warm and affectionate, we heard a clear voice, which disarmed all my ceremonial sentences, that made us feel at ease, happy and relaxed: — Welcome Brazilian friends! It was Mussolini's voice. Good and simple. It is the figure of the Duce, modest and affectionate. He is the greatest figure in contemporary Europe, and who forms, with Lenin and Gandhi, the great triptych of humanity today, he makes himself little in private, or perhaps greater, because all greatness is simple... [...] Mussolini is emotive. I watched him in certain parts of our conversation. The sign of a genius.]

One sees the admiration that Plínio Salgado had for Mussolini. In the article, the Brazilian integralist leader made his desire for Brazil explicit: to create a fascist movement, like the Italian one: 'Nós éramos o Brasil-Novo que ia falar à Itália ressuscitada no esplendor de uma juventude de primavera. A doutrina corrente entre os moços da nossa Pátria coincidia, nas suas linhas gerais, com os largos lineamentos da ideia fascista' [We were the New-Brazil, who were going to talk to the resuscitated Italy in the splendor of a youth of spring. The current doctrine among the youths of our country coincided, in general terms, with the broad guidelines of the fascist idea].[70]

In a later article in *Revista Hierarchia*, the author raised Italy to a level of superiority: 'A Itália que eu vi merece todo o amor do Homem deste século de ameaças' [The Italy that I saw deserves all the love of Mankind in this century of threats].[71] He placed Mussolini in a position of privilege for having put fascism into practice and he reports that the 'meeting' — of fifteen minutes — was a unique moment in his life, because he had experience contact with profound wisdom:

Numa tarde de junho, depois de ter visto toda a Itália Nova, depois de a ter julgado com todo o rigor, eu me vi, no Palácio de Venezia, frente a frente com o gênio criador da política do Futuro. Era um homem de estatura regular, de olhos azuis, de gestos seguros e de voz firme. E esse gesto e essa voz pareciam exprimir uma concepção de vida. Por eram quentes e queriam ser impetuosos, como afirmações violentas de personalidade individual; porém, eram ao mesmo tempo, brando e refletidos, e se condicionavam numa perfeita expressão de ponderada disciplina. Por vezes, no correr da palestra, aqueles olhos se iluminavam, como se perpassasse por ele a chama de um ideal superior; e, em seguida, como se cerravam levemente, dir-se-

---

[70]   Salgado, 'Como eu vi a Itália', p. 205.
[71]   Ibid.

ia que a retomar um ritmo que constitui toda a sabedoria de uma raça. Esse homem, de expressão vigorosa, tinha uma máscara inconfundível, onde velhos sofrimentos e velhas lutas pareciam ter marcado a passagem de uma vida agitada e forte. Era o homem que viera do seio das multidões com a luz do gênio latino, médium supremo da nacionalidade, profeta das Nações e contemporâneo do Futuro. Era Mussolini. [...] Esse homem criará a Nova Itália, mas não ficará ali. Cidadão da Humanidade oferecerá aos Povos angustiados o conteúdo ideológico do Estado que deverá constituir a essência dos princípios políticos dos países que preferirem uma Humanidade humana a uma Humanidade mecânica.[72]

[On an afternoon in June, after seeing the whole of New Italy, after having judged it with full rigour, I found myself at the Palazzo di Venezia, face to face with the creative genius of the politics of the Future. He was a man of average height, with blue eyes, confident gestures, and a firm voice. And this gesture and voice seemed to express a conception of life. Because they were warm and longed to be impetuous, as violent assertions of an individual personality, but were at the same time soft and reflective, and were conditions for a perfect expression of considered discipline. Occasionally, in the course of the conversation, those eyes would light up, as if he were pierced with the flame of a higher ideal, and then, as if closing slightly, seeming to resume a rhythm that constitutes all the wisdom of a race. This man of vigorous expression had a distinctive mask, where old sufferings and old struggles seemed to have marked the passage of a hectic and forceful lifestyle. He was the man who had come from the bosom of the crowds with the light of the Latin genius, a supreme medium of the nation, a prophet of Nations and a contemporary of the Future. It was Mussolini. [...] This man will create the New Italy, but he will not stop there. A citizen of Humanity, he will provide for the anguished People the ideological content of the State, which should be the essence of the political principles of countries that prefer a humane Humanity to a mechanical Humanity.]

The need to create something solid in Brazil prompted him to look to Italy. It is understandable that the author exalts the Italian fascist regime, but while he saw fascism as a marker to be followed, he also saw the need for a movement based on originality:

Lembro-me bem das palavras da minha despedida. Mussolini lera no meu olhar o meu grande amor pelo Brasil. Augurou-me os mais completos triunfos a mocidade do meu país. E concitando-me a não esmorecer no entusiasmo e na fé pelo futuro do Brasil, pediu-me que fizesse justiça a sua Itália. [...] Foi assim que eu compreendi, foi assim que eu vi a Itália.[73]

[I remember well the words of farewell. Mussolini had read in my eyes my great love for Brazil. He augured me the most complete triumphs to the youth of my country. And urging me to not weaken in enthusiasm and faith in the future of Brazil, he asked me to do justice to his Italy. [...] That is how I understood it, that was how I saw Italy.]

[72] Ibid.
[73] Ibid.

With this view, the author initiated the practical implementation of nationalist thought, and around such thoughts sought the birth of a new and necessary political culture corresponding to emergence of new concepts: 'às respostas dadas a uma sociedade face aos grandes problemas e às grandes crises da sua história, respostas com fundamento bastante para que se inscrevam na duração e atravessem as gerações' [to the answers given to a society facing the great problems and major crises in its history, responses with a sufficient foundation to last through time and pass across the generations].[74]

In late February 1932, the Sociedade de Estudos Políticos [Society of Political Studies] (SEP) was founded,[75] a body that was a result of the political work conducted by the newspaper *A Razão*. The idea was to form a group which could discuss the creation of a new political movement based on the principle of a strong conservative and revolutionary nationalism, thus following Mussolini's proposal. It was the result of several other movements that had existed in Brazil in previous years, groups that can be termed pre-foundational, notably the Ação Imperial Patrionovista Brasileira (AIPB), a neo-monarchist Catholic organization created to restore the monarchy in Brazil, following the medievalist characteristics found in a Royal Catholic structures. With this movement, Plínio Salgado began to shape more clearly the ideas that would become part of the structuring of the AIB.

The AIPB has a fundamental importance for the development of the political structure supporting the integralist movement in Brazil, because it was through the encouragement of Brazilian monarchism that the ideals based on the Catholic and monarchist discourse of Integralismo Lusitano arrived in the country. The cultural reflection of the Portuguese movement appeared 'inicialmente em movimentos de cariz monárquico como a Ação Imperial Patrionovista Brasileira, criada em 1928' [initially in movements with a monarchical aspect, such as the Ação Imperial Patrionovista Brasileira, created in 1928].[76]

Besides his characterization of the AIB as a Brazilian fascist movement in his work *Integralismo e o mundo*, Gustavo Barroso analysed the political programme of *patrionovismo*, explaining: 'O *Patrionovismo* é monarquista, porque é integralista' [*Patrionovismo* is monarchist, because it is integralist].[77] The relation of proximity between the two political processes is evident:[78]

---

[74]   Serge Berstein, 'A cultura política', in *Para uma história cultural*, ed. by Jean-Pierre Rioux and Jean-François Sirinelli (Lisbon: Estampa, 1998), pp. 349–63 (p. 355).
[75]   The founding meeting SEP took place on 24 February 1932, on the initiative of Salgado, in São Paulo, in the newsroom of *A Razão*. A group of young intellectuals took part in this meeting: Cândido Mota Filho, Ataliba Nogueira, Mário Graciotti, João Leães Sobrinho, Fernando Callage and several students from the School of Law. Trindade, *Integralismo*, p. 116.
[76]   Pinto, *Os Camisas Azuis*, p. 144.
[77]   Barroso, *Integralismo e o mundo*, p. 43.
[78]   Alongside his theoretical sympathies, Plínio Salgado proved to be an admirer of the Lusitanian movement, because besides evidence of numerous contacts with members of the Portuguese counterpart, several clippings and materials of the Integralists were located in the Fundo Plínio Salgado in the Arquivo Público e Histórico de Rio Claro, among them poems by António Sardinha and texts by Alberto de Monsaraz. Cf. António Sardinha, 'Poema do cavalo', *Acção*, April 1945 (Arquivo

'o brasileiro, posterior ao português, foi expressamente influenciado por este' [the Brazilian [movement], subsequent to the Portuguese, was explicitly influenced by the latter].[79] However, this research does not claim that the Brazilian integralist movement embraced a defence of monarchism, like its Lusitanian counterpart, although in the 1920s it maintained good relations with the monarchical regime. Unlike many, the integralist leader did not develop great discourses in opposition to the monarchy, despite being a fierce critic of the monarchical model that existed in Brazil until 1889. In a lecture delivered on 23 May 1937,[80] in Rio de Janeiro, he criticized federalism in defence of the Integral State and condemned the regime of Dom Pedro II on account of its centralization of political power in the Emperor: the 'poder pessoal do Monarca era nocivo' [personal power of the Monarch was harmful].[81] If the figure of the Emperor did not offer a model capable of inspiring a mystique around the throne, the ideal image of governance

> [...] foi calcada na monarquia portuguesa e mais concretamente em Afonso Henriques, fundador da nacionalidade portuguesa e associado a uma profecia, a mesma difundida pelo *Integralismo Lusitano*, de que sobre a descendência desse personagem seria fundado um grande Império, época de progresso incomparável da nação católica.[82]

> [was based on the Portuguese monarchy and more precisely on Afonso Henriques, the founder of the Portuguese nationality and associated with a prophecy, itself disseminated by *Integralismo Lusitano*, that on the lineage of this character would be established a great Empire, a time of unparalleled progress of the Catholic nation.]

The research does not claim that the Brazilian integralist movement included a defence of the monarchy, like its Lusitanian counterpart, although in the 1920s Plínio Salgado enjoyed good relations with the monarchical regime. The relationship between the Lusitanian integralists and the AIPB was a very intense one, including the promotion of cultural and ideological exchanges between the groups. In the journal *Integralismo Lusitano: estudos portugueses*, directed by Luís de Almeida Braga and Hipólito Raposo, there were messages of support for the struggle of Brazilian neo-monarchists in defence of the doctrine elaborated within Integralismo Lusitano:

Público e Histórico de Rio Claro/Fundo Plínio Salgado — APHRC/FPS-107.002); Alberto Monsaraz (under the pseudonym Évora Macedo), 'A Monarquia Futura I, II, III e IV', *O Jornal do Comércio e das Colónias*, 14, 15, 16, 21 May 1947; Alberto Monsaraz (under the pseudonym Évora Macedo), 'Atlântico e Liberdade', *O Jornal do Comércio e das Colónias*, 26 May 1947 (APHRC/FPS-109.004).

[79]   Ubiratan Borges de Macedo, 'O integralismo em Portugal e no Brasil', *Convivium*, 28 (1983), 323–40 (p. 323).

[80]   The text was also reprinted in Plínio Salgado, *Livro verde da minha campanha* (Rio de Janeiro: Clássica brasileira, 1956), pp. 209–24, but with the date of 29 May 1937.

[81]   Plínio Salgado, 'Salvemos a Democracia!', *O integralismo perante a nação*, 2nd edn (Rio de Janeiro: Clássica brasileira, 1950), p. 89.

[82]   Malatian, *Império e missão*, p. 137.

Patrionovismo: com esta designação iniciou-se há poucos anos no Brasil um movimento de ideias político-sociais, destinado a instaurar nos costumes a ordem cristã e latina e a reconduzir a Pátria-Irmã ao caminho perdido da sua Grandeza pela restauração do Império, na pessoa do príncipe Dom Pedro Henrique de Orleans e Bragança. Movimento da mocidade já doutrinada nos princípios antiliberais e antidemocráticos, norteia-o a certeza de que é essencial à conservação da unidade do Brasil a existência de um poder político, forte, contínuo e seguramente nacional nas suas intenções, que não possa ser escravo do partido da maioria, por ficar sobranceiro a todas as facções. Alheios à política do Brasil, como devemos ser, nada nos impede de saudar a grande esperança que a sua juventude põe nos mesmos princípios de salvação pública por que há vinte anos vimos lutando, em obediência à lei do sacrifício pelo bem-comum. Aos rapazes patrionovistas, os integralistas da grande e querida Nação-Irmã, enviamos os mais afetuosos votos e a melhor lembrança de apreço aos órgãos dos seus centros [...] agradecendo a todos as palavras com que acolheram o *Integralismo Lusitano*.[83]

[*Patrionovismo*: a few years ago in Brazil, a movement of political and social ideas with this designation was initiated with the aim of establishing in our morals the Latin and Christian order and leading the Sister-Homeland back to the lost path of its Greatness, by the restoration of the Empire, in the person of Prince Dom Pedro Henrique de Orleans e Bragança. It is a youth movement which is already indoctrinated in anti-liberal and anti-democratic principles and it is guided by the certainty that it is essential to the preservation of the unity of Brazil to have a political power which is strong, solid and assuredly national in its intentions, which cannot be a slave to the party of the majority because it dominates all factions. External to the politics of Brazil, as we should be, nothing prevents us from hailing the great hope that its youth places in the same principles of public salvation that for twenty years we have been fighting for in obedience to the law of sacrifice for the collective wellbeing. To the *Patrionovista* boys, the integralists of the great and beloved Sister-Nation, we send our most affectionate wishes, and a special reminder of appreciation to their centres' periodicals [...] thanking all of them for the words with which they embraced *Integralismo Lusitano*.]

Brazilian integralism owed its choice of the republican path to Miguel Reale.[84] Within the AIB there were several disagreements over the political terrain, especially between Plínio Salgado, Gustavo Barroso and Miguel Reale. The last of these headed the Departamento Nacional de Doutrina and, in turn, had the control of various political mechanisms disseminated in the movement. Unlike Plínio Salgado, Reale did not approve of monarchist movements: 'O republicanismo e um certo preconceito antifrancês explica sua atitude com relação à Ação Francesa e ao Integralismo, ambos monarquistas'

---

[83] 'Res et Verba', in *Integralismo Lusitano: estudos portugueses*, ed. by Luís de Almeida Braga and Hipólito Raposo (Lisbon: Tip. Inglesa, 1932–34), pp. 250–51.
[84] Trindade, *Integralismo*, p. 251.

[Republicanism and a certain anti-French prejudice explain his attitude toward the Action Française and Integralism, both monarchist].[85]

When analysing the absolutist king D. José I's Prime Minister, the Marquis of Pombal, the integralists stated: 'Por afirmar que o *absolutismo* não era uma forma política reprovável e que não se podia confundir com o *despotismo* ou a *tirania*' [By declaring that absolutism was not an objectionable political form and that it should not be confused with *despotism* or *tyranny*].[86] The integralist group

> [...] deseja provar que na nossa monarquia, salvo raras exceções, não houve 'absolutismo', pois os reis procuraram sempre respeitar as leis existentes e as liberdades do povo português. No liberalismo é que, efetivamente, houve 'absolutismo', pois calcaram-se as leis legitimas da monarquia. Esta foi, de fato, a ideia apresentada pelos integralistas, que distinguiram 'poder pessoal', que o rei tem efetivamente de assumir, e 'poder absoluto', que constitui já um vício. [...] É neste contexto teórico — de combate, é certo, mas já fora do ambiente polêmico pombalino de 1782 — que temos de entender a posição integralista em relação ao Ministro de D. José. Ela vai considerar que o 'poder absoluto' só existiu em Portugal no tempo de Pombal. [...] Diga-se, porém, como complemento, que não era o integralismo, movimento de raiz miguelista, o único setor monárquico que então tomara posição contra as manifestações em honra de Pombal.[87]

> [wishes to prove that in our monarchy, with rare exceptions, there was no 'absolutism' because the kings sought always to respect the existing laws and fundamental freedoms of the Portuguese people. It was in liberalism that effectively there was 'absolutism', as it trampled on the legitimate laws of the monarchy. This was, in fact, the idea presented by the integralists, that distinguished between 'personal power', which the king has effectively to assume, and 'absolute power', which already constituted a vice. [...] It is in this theoretical context — of combat, of course, but already out of the polemical environment of 1782 under Pombal — that we have to understand the fundamentalist position in relation to D. José's Minister. It considers that 'absolute power' only existed in Portugal at the time of Pombal. [...] Let it be said, however, as a complement, that integralism, a movement rooted in Miguelism, was not the only monarchical sector which then took a stance against the celebrations in honour of Pombal.]

From this point of view, it is far easier to grasp the fact that the goal of the Integralismo Lusitano was not merely to promote the national restoration of the monarchical period but rather, to create an element that would justify the need to regain the Portugal of the so-called 'golden times' in the process described as medieval. António Sardinha put it thus: 'é de uso corrente reputar-se à Idade Média como um eclipse duradouro da inteligência humana, só ressuscitada do seu sono longuíssimo pelos clarões vitoriosos da Renascença. A calúnia da

[85] Ibid.
[86] Luís Reis Torgal, *História e ideologia* (Coimbra: Minerva História, 1989), p. 84.
[87] Torgal, p. 87.

Idade Média é a calúnia contra a Igreja' [it is customary to refer to the Middle Ages as a long-lasting eclipse of human intelligence, only resurrected from its extremely long slumber by the victorious flashes of the Renaissance. A calumny against the Middle Ages is a calumny against the Church].[88] That is to say, the medieval values of nationalist defence were associated, according to Plínio Salgado, with a Christian practice. This way of thinking led him to state that: 'Construir uma Pátria é muito difícil. [...] Porque uma Nação pode ser uma obra política, mas uma Pátria é uma arquitetura moral e espiritual' [Building a Homeland is very difficult. [...] Because a Nation can be a political work, but a Homeland is a moral and spiritual architecture].[89] To think of nationalism with religious practice was the approach he advocated when speaking to militants in defence of the relationship between national feeling and Christian thought. In an interview with the *Correio da Manhã* he stated:

> Despertar em si próprio as forças do sentimento nacional porque a fusão de todas as centelhas de patriotismo de cada coração formará fogueira que incendiará o grande coração da Pátria Total. Pedir a Deus coragem e paciência, fortaleza e inspiração, energia e bondade, severidade sem alarde, bravura sem ostentação, virtude sem orgulho puritanista, humildade sem indignidade e dignidade sem egolatria.[90]

> [To awaken in oneself the forces of national feeling because the fusion of all the sparks of patriotism in every heart will form a fire that will set the great heart of the Homeland alight. To ask God for courage and patience, fortitude and inspiration, energy and kindness, severity without fuss, bravery without ostentation, virtue without puritanical pride, humility without indignity and dignity without egotism.]

The spiritual renaissance was a movement that appeared under French influence, with the objective of restoring spiritual values in poetry, prose and philosophy. 'Este movimento de espiritualização dos intelectuais é marcado, como o da França, no início do século, por um espírito antimoderno, antiburguês pela nostalgia da Idade Média' [This movement of spiritualization of intellectuals is marked, like that of France, at the beginning of the century, by an anti-modern spirit, anti-bourgeois out of nostalgia for the Middle Ages].[91]

With the establishment of the AIB and the undisputed leadership of Plínio Salgado, 'tornou-se insuperável a divergência entre patrionovistas e plinistas' [the divergence between *patrionovistas* and *plinistas* became insuperable].[92] The differences between the AIPB and the AIB were very clear and incapable of sustaining a fully articulated relationship between the groups. The separation established between them did not mean opposition,

---

[88] António Sardinha, *A teoria das cortes gerais*, 2nd edn (Lisbon: qp, 1975), p. 20.
[89] Plínio Salgado, 'O drama dos constructores de pátrias', in *Palavra nova dos tempos novos* (Rio de Janeiro: José Olympio, 1936), pp. 15–18.
[90] Plínio Salgado, 'Sentido e rythmo da nossa revolução', *A doutrina do Sigma* (São Paulo: Revista dos Tribunais, 1935), p. 18.
[91] Trindade, *Integralismo*, p. 30.
[92] Malatian, *Império e missão*, p. 67.

however. On several occasions, the Brazilian *patrionovistas* (who were fewer in numbers) demonstrated support for the integralists, especially with regard to discourses around corporatist social practice within a Christian precept of ideas originating from *Action Française* and Integralismo Lusitano. A clear example took place during the presidential election of 1955, in which Plínio Salgado was a candidate. The newspaper *Monarquia: órgão da chefia geral patrionovista* stated in a note: 'Presidência da República — Confirmando por este meio os comunicados anteriores, o Chefe Geral Patrionovista, Com. Prof. Dr. Arlindo Veiga dos Santos, aconselha aos patrionovistas e outros monárquicos não filiados à A.I.P.B. a candidatura de Plínio Salgado' [The Presidency of the Republic — Confirming by this means the previous announcements, the Patrionovista General Leader, Com. Prof. Dr. Arlindo Veiga dos Santos, advises *patrionovistas* and other monarchists not affiliated with A.I.P.B. to vote for Plínio Salgado].[93]

Through this relationship, the Franco-Lusitanian elements consolidated Plínio Salgado's thinking on Brazilian extreme conservatism. To identify the intellectual conception contained in this fundamentalist movement, we have had to analyse the movement of greatest inspiration for the Brazilian leader, Integralismo Lusitano, as influenced by *Action Française*, and the practical experience of Italian fascism, based on the Social Doctrine of the church. These movements provided a basis for the political construction of a fascist organization in the guise of Christian nationalism, whose sole purpose was to achieve supreme power around the undisputed leadership of Plínio Salgado, who would be able to assume the 'real' role that did not actually exist in Republican Brazil. In 1937 the AIB was extinguished by a dictatorial decree issued by Getúlio Vargas, culminating in the exile of Plínio Salgado to Portugal from 1939 onwards. Through this direct contact with Salgado, Lusitanian conservatism brought about a doctrinal reorientation in the political thinking of the integralist leader, who went on to draw up new directives in 1946 when he returned to Brazil. Via Catholicism Plínio Salgado was strongly attracted to Salazarist politics; he became known as a 'Luso-Brazilian' for his affinities with the corporatist matrix exemplified in the Portuguese model, a dimension of his thinking to which he held on until his death in 1975.

---

[93] *Monarquia: órgão da chefia geral patrionovista*, 3 (October 1955) (Arquivo Nacional da Torre do Tombo/Arquivo Oliveira Salazar — ANTT/AOS/PC-3R).

The Question of the Political Organization of Catholics under the Portuguese Authoritarian Regime: The 'Bishop of Porto Case' (1958)

Paula Borges Santos

Instituto de História Contemporânea,
Universidade Nova de Lisboa

The Political Demobilization of Catholics: A Government Strategy

Throughout the period of the *Estado Novo*, between 1933 and 1974, the strategy of a political demobilization of Catholics was one of the main guiding principles adopted by the civil authorities in the face of religious forces in Portugal. During this whole time the government rejected the idea of political autonomy for Catholics, restricting the possibility for an organized intervention to the sphere of the *União Nacional* (renamed, in 1970, *Acção Nacional Popular*). The prohibition of political activity outside the *União Nacional* was not directed exclusively at Catholics, but towards all groups with political aims and capacities. The extinction of the *Movimento Nacional-Sindicalista*, for example, was a result of this policy, and in fact the only exception was that made for the *Causa Monárquica*. Even so, as we shall see below, the policy created more problems than it solved in the government's aim to prevent the state being fragmented along party lines. Moreover, the existence of this state imposition did not at any point in the regime dispose of the problem of the political responsibilities of individual Catholics and of their intervention in society. There were moments that were more favourable to the interests of the government forces, as was the case in the 1930s, with the progressive deactivation of the Catholic political party, the so-called *Centro Católico Português* (CCP), and others less favourable, particularly after the Second World War, when the government's attitude was repeatedly put in question. This hindered the process of compromise with the different Catholic groups (including those that gravitated towards the government's sphere of influence), which were increasingly involved in public life and determined to fight for leadership and influence (not only in the name of the church's interests, but also in defence of their own political ideologies). From 1958 onwards the government attempted to demobilize and confront the different Catholic groups that entered into ideological and programmatic conflict with the regime, not hesitating to resort to the repressive mechanisms of the state, such as prior censorship and use of the political police.

Portuguese Studies vol. 30 no. 1 (2014), 94–111

Salazar kept a particularly close eye on two Catholic organizations, the CCP and the *Ação Católica Portuguesa* (ACP), fearing that they could evolve to become confessional parties. For this reason he favoured a downgrading of the CCP, exploiting the tactical and strategic weakness that that party had shown since the late 1920s, the result of a dispute that divided its supporters between its being a 'partido de defesa cristã' [party for the defence of Christianity] and a 'partido de governo e cristão' [party of government and Christianity]; Salazar suggested that it be transformed into a 'vasto organismo dedicado à ação social' [vast organism devoted to social intervention]. This suggestion showed that Salazar was in tune with the new thinking of the papacy, which at the time was backing the creation of branches of Catholic Action to the detriment of confessional parties, though in his case with an aim of narrow political convenience. In reality, by his proposal Salazar was safeguarding his personal position in power, and the preponderance of the Executive in the formulation of religious policy and the regulation of political movements.

The ecclesiastical authorities, however, only agreed to shut down the CCP in 1940, after obtaining confirmation that a concordat would be celebrated that year between the Holy See and Portugal.[1] Their action is understandable in light of the strategy of the Portuguese episcopate and the Holy See to keep hold of an instrument with which they could exert some pressure on the government. The retention of the Centre represented the threat that, in the event that they did not secure from the state a favourable agreement on the juridical position of the church in Portugal, the religious authorities would be able to restart the political struggle against the government in defence of religious liberty.[2] Retaining the CCP also allowed the episcopate to avoid, for the time being, a confrontation with certain sections of Catholics who still saw a value in the autonomy of that structure, and who supported its retention in order to defend the interests of the Catholic Church.[3] Since the opportunity offered by the creation of the ACP had not been taken to close down the Centre, any action in this direction would seem with hindsight to be particularly senseless, as long as the religious authorities had been unable to announce publicly that they were negotiating a concordat.

As for the ACP, the control that Salazar sought to exercise over that organization, created in 1933, resulted in there being no reference to it in the

[1] The CCP was formally closed down in January 1940, five months before the signing of the Concordat. Until that time, its activities had centred on providing legal assistance and administrative support to the clergy and the corporations representing the Catholic faith. The CCP's periodical, *A União*, had ceased publication in February 1939. See Paula Borges Santos, 'A política religiosa do Estado Novo (1933–1974): estado, leis, governação e interesses religiosos' (unpublished doctoral thesis, Faculdade de Ciências Sociais e Humanas, Universidade Nova de Lisboa, November 2012), pp. 294–300.
[2] Cf. Rita Almeida de Carvalho, *A Concordata de Salazar* (Lisbon: Círculo de Leitores and Temas e Debates, 2013), pp. 384–94.
[3] Cf. Historical archive of José Maria Braga da Cruz: newspaper cutting from *Correio do Minho*, 23 November 1933, p. 1; meeting of the Braga Diocesan Commission of the CCP, held on 20 November 1933.

Concordat of 1940, and at no point in its life cycle did the ACP achieve any legal status, whether civil or even canonical. From a political point of view it remained advantageous to the Executive that the ACP should not be recognized canonically, which would result in the state being obliged to give it recognition in civil law. The existence of the ACP without proper civil status, and subject only to the civil law governing unrecognized associations, widened the state's margin for manoeuvre over the organization, if its members should choose to engage in political activity. Freed in this way from giving special treatment to the organizations of the ACP, the government took advantage of a situation in which Catholics could count only on its tolerance towards the activities that they wished to engage in.

The Portuguese Episcopate and the Problem of the
Freedom of Political Activity for Catholics

The government's strategy towards the CCP and the ACP, as well as averting a political mobilization by some of their members in ways unfavourable to the regime, proved to be effective in shaping the behaviour of the ecclesiastical authorities, who did not encourage Catholic initiatives that might reproduce a party structure, and opted instead to distance themselves from any criticism or activities launched by Catholic elements in opposition to the government's political project.

In order to uphold this position, which in practice was related to its efforts to safeguard the areas of autonomy that the church enjoyed in society and to avoid the state's raising objections to the activities and organizations amongst Catholics that existed in a number of fields, but mainly in education and social assistance, the episcopate incorporated its own attitude into the ACP's approach to Catholics' relationship to politics: the maintenance of a policy of abstention from 'concrete politics'. However, the ACP's approach recognized the right of Catholics to political activity in a personal capacity,[4] and in this respect laid the

---

[4]   The logic behind the Pontificate's project for the creation of the ACP was to supersede the model of Christian intervention in society by way of confessional parties, but it was not clear, in political terms, what was meant by the organization's intention of acting 'fora e acima de todas as correntes políticas, sem deixar de reivindicar e defender as liberdades da Igreja' [outside and above all political currents, while still laying claim to and defending the freedoms of the church] (article IV.1 of the programme of the ACP). The principles governing the conduct of activists of the ACP's component organizations were also open to different interpretations, by making distinctions between the political behaviour of the members and of their leaders. On the one hand, it was established that the governing bodies of the ACP could not 'fazer parte indivíduos que exerçam atividade incompatível com a independência política da mesma' [include individuals who exercised activities incompatible with its political independence]; while for members, on the other hand, there was admission to the ACP of 'todos os católicos' [all Catholics], 'independentemente dos seus ideais políticos' [independently of their political ideas] (articles IV.3 and IV.2). The difference lay in the suggestion that the former were obliged to safeguard the political independence of *Ação Católica*, accepting an implicit formal restriction on their personal freedom of political activity, while the latter enjoyed a recognized freedom of choice in terms of political ideology. In a situation where the guiding criteria did not appear to be clearly defined, or

basis for the ecclesiastical and political tensions that not only led to a challenge to the episcopate's position towards public engagement by some Catholic groups, particularly after the war, but also led to the conflict that, in 1958, put the Bishop of Porto, D. António Ferreira Gomes, at loggerheads with Salazar.

The understanding that the episcopate made of the principle that Catholics, individually, enjoyed freedom of political activity, was developed within the framework of a political intervention by believers nevertheless structured according to the guiding principle of the church's interests in society.[5] This meant that the prelates believed that there existed 'o dever de obediência dos católicos' [a duty of obedience by Catholics] to the norms dictated by the ecclesiastical authorities regarding political activity, and that these involved, principally, the following obligations: 'de resistir às leis quando a autoridade manda alguma coisa injusta' [to resist laws when the civil authority ordains something unjust]; to collaborate with the constituted powers that aim to defend the 'observância da lei divina e dos direitos da Igreja na vida particular e pública' [observance of divine law and of the rights of the church in private and in public life], by applying the church's social doctrine 'ao serviço do bem comum' [for the service of the common good]; and 'não enfeudar politicamente a Igreja' [not compromise the church politically] (that is, it was forbidden to use the term 'Catholic' to designate confessional political activities or organizations without the approval of the religious authorities).[6] In line with this way of thinking, throughout the 1950s, the episcopate renewed its condemnation of Marxism, as an ideology that 'nega a missão e a liberdade da Igreja e sacrifica os direitos da pessoa no altar do Estado, ou da classe ou do povo' [rejects the

even seemed contradictory, their interpretation could only be settled by the ecclesiastical authorities, who, under these circumstances, were at liberty to decide what belonged to the domain of religion, and what to politics. (Cf. Paulo Fontes, *Elites católicas em Portugal: o papel da Acção Católica (1940–1961)* (Lisbon: Fundação Calouste Gulbenkian/ Fundação para a Ciência e a Tecnologia, 2011), pp. 449–50).

[5] It should be noted that the idea of political organization by Catholics in order to intervene in public life, with the aim of securing Catholic demands, arose in Portugal, as happened in various European countries, and with the encouragement of the Holy See, in the last quarter of the nineteenth century. From that time, and up to the end of the First Republic (1926), that idea was mostly achieved through projects for the creation of confessional parties, albeit on different models (the *Centro Católico Parlamentar*, for example, created in 1894, had been a platform bringing together Catholic deputies from different parties). The *Centro Católico Português* corresponded to the final political structure created with that strategy in mind. *Ação Católica* broke for the first time with that model of party organization by refusing to work specifically as a party, but it in no way rejected the idea that Catholics needed to defend the interests of the church in public life, and specifically in the political sphere. For an overview of the Portuguese situation, see Manuel Braga da Cruz, 'Partidos Políticos Confessionais', in *Dicionário de história religiosa de Portugal*, ed. by Carlos Moreira Azevedo (Rio de Mouro: Círculo de Leitores, 2001), vol. III, pp. 380–82. For a broad discussion of the different European cases see Martin Conway, *Catholic Politics in Europe (1918–1945)* (London: Routledge, 1997), pp. 11–77; and Jean-Marie Mayeur, *Des partis catholiques à la Démocratie chrétienne (XIX–XX siècles)* (Paris: Armand Colin), pp. 17–160).

[6] Cf. D. Manuel Gonçalves Cerejeira, 'A posição da Igreja e dos católicos perante a política', in *Lumen*, vol. IX, December 1945, p. 729; Idem, 'Na festa litúrgica de Cristo-Rei', in *Obras Pastorais*, VII vol., Lisbon, União Gráfica, p. 729; *Boletim de Acção Católica Portuguesa*, 'Os católicos e a vida pública', nos 313–14, July-August 1960, pp. 78–79; Idem, «Ação católica e ação política», no. 185, p. 110.

mission and the freedom of the church and sacrifices the rights of the individual on the altar of the state, or of class or of the people], renewing the prohibition upon believers of allying themselves 'na empresa política, com aqueles que negam Cristo, e querem destruir, ou pelo menos encadear e emudecer a Igreja' [in political activity, with those who deny Christ, and wish to destroy, or at least to shackle or silence the church].[7] In adopting this position, which echoes the condemnation that Cardinal Cerejeira and the Portuguese bishops made of communism and the totalitarian state at the end of the 1930s,[8] the ecclesiastical hierarchy insisted upon the view that the best defence against the danger of communism in Portugal was still the Salazar regime. This stance by the religious authorities remained constant throughout the episcopacy of Cardinal Cerejeira, but went into crisis from 1958, as a result of the presidential elections, and more particularly of the conflict between political and religious authorities that arose from the memorandum that the Bishop of Porto, D. António Ferreira Gomes, sent to Salazar, in the summer of that year.

Differences within the Episcopate: An Alternative Understanding of the Political Activity of Catholics as Defended by the Bishop of Porto, in 1958

The memorandum that D. António Ferreira Gomes sent to Salazar, on 13 July 1958, is understandable within the climate of political and social crisis created by the presidential elections that year, which were marked not only by an increasing number of Christians backing the opposition, but also by many Catholics, traditionally supporters of the Government, expressing criticism of the political system and the economic and social situation in Portugal, and giving support to the Executive with the expectation of subsequent social and institutional reforms.

In his memorandum, the Bishop of Porto dealt separately with two topics. He devoted the first part to social problems, while in the second he went on to deal with the political problem resulting from one of the regime's guiding principles regarding the relationship between politics and religion, namely the rejection of any idea of freedom of political organization for Catholics. The Bishop's observations on social questions included criticism of the civil authorities' refusal to recognize the right to strike, and the preference given to corporative organization; an identification of the problem of low salaries, a failure to distribute the rewards of labour fairly, and the growth of unemployment; and denunciations of working conditions that violated the rights of workers and of the increase in hardship amongst rural workers. These remarks were

---

[7] Cf. 'Nota Coletiva do Episcopado Português ao "Programa para a democratização da República"', in *Lumen*, vol. XXV, December 1961, pp. 1070–71.
[8] Cf. 'Pastoral coletiva sobre o comunismo e alguns problemas da hora presente', in *Lumen*, vol. I, 1937, pp. 209–26; D. Manuel Gonçalves Cerejeira, 'Ação Católica e Política', in *Obras Pastorais*, vol. II, 2nd edition (Lisbon: União Gráfica, 1961), pp. 161–78.

unwelcome to Salazar, given that the Bishop was distancing himself from government policy, but they hardly represented any novelty.[9]

It was in its approach to political matters, though, that the Bishop's memorandum caused the most difficulties for Salazar, who regarded it as unacceptable because he took it as encouraging the formation of a Catholic force as a political alternative to the model of the regime. The Bishop had aroused the greatest concern in government circles since the formation of the ACP, not only by failing to condemn the political activity of Catholics, in rejecting the notion that the church could allow believers to be subjected to the doctrine according to which 'o cidadão português não precisa de ter dimensão política' [the Portuguese citizen does not need to have a political dimension], but also by questioning 'a escala de valores adotada e mantida' [the scale of values adopted and upheld], and the Constitution itself, which removed 'a liberdade de formação da opinião pública' [the freedom to shape public opinion] and reduced 'a vida política à Administração' [political life to the Administration], transforming it into 'toda ou quase toda a ideologia prática' [all, or practically all the practical ideology] of the regime, where 'o homem não tem que pensar em realizar-se politicamente' [man cannot think of fulfilling himself politically]. The essential problem for the Bishop of Porto was the 'negação da livre e honesta atividade política' [denial of free and honest political activity]; a 'má política' [bad policy] that was reflected in the establishing of the União Nacional, which, D. António wrote, either 'não tem qualquer doutrina e então temos [...] a negação da dimensão política, ou bem que tem uma doutrina e nesse caso, ou é dogmática e estamos no mesmo, ou é livre e caímos na sua negação, na desunião' [either has no doctrine, and so we have a denial of the political dimension, or it has a doctrine and in that case either it is dogmatic and we are in the same position, or it is open and we fall into its negation, into disunity]. Further regarding the aims of the União Nacional and the behaviour that it saw as being required of its members, the prelate questioned the legitimacy of imposing on Catholics conformity with the nationalist politics followed by the Portuguese state,

[9] In reality, the social question had been the subject of discussion and criticism within the Catholic camp since the formalization of the Estado Novo by the Constitution of 1933. From the second half of the 1930s various Catholic forces and some organizations within Ação Católica had expressed disagreement with the statist orientation given to social policy and the corporativist project, and voices of discontent had increased during the years of the Second World War. About a year earlier, in April 1957, the Bishop of Porto himself had criticized various aspects of socioeconomic organization, and described the position of rural workers as 'miséria imerecida' [undeserved misery]. Nor had such criticisms, touching on the problem of relations between the state and the corporative organization, been restricted to Catholic circles; from the final years of the War onwards they were made not only by critics of the regime but also by various supporters of the Estado Novo, some of them important figures in corporative policy making and activities. (Cf. Novidades, 3 May 1937, p. 1; 7 February 1939, p. 3; 6 February 1941, p. 6; 14 February 1941, pp. 1 and 6; 3 March 1941, pp. 1 and 4; 20, 24, 25, 26, 28, 29 April and 1 May 1957, pp. 1–5. The newspaper Novidades, founded in 1923 and closed in 1974 by decision of the Portuguese Episcopal Conference, was a Catholic daily paper which functioned as the official organ of the Portuguese episcopate; see Manuel de Lucena, 'Salazar, António de Oliveira', in Dicionário de História de Portugal: suplemento, ed. by António Barreto and Maria Filomena Mónica (Lisbon/Porto: Livraria Figueirinhas, 1999), vol. IX, pp. 300–01.)

recalling to that end that Pope Pius XII, in his 1954 Christmas radio broadcast, had condemned the nationalist politics exercised by the 'strong state'. In the face of what he took to be the political inflexibility of the regime, the Bishop of Porto saw a growing danger of an 'irrupção anarco-social-comunista' [an anarcho-social-communist outburst] and he did not see how it was possible for the 'forças da civilização' [forces of civilization] to stand that 'embate' [shock] without unity on the 'frente cristã' [Christian front].[10] To achieve that unity there was only one legitimate avenue: that of avoiding the instrumentalization of Catholics in support of the regime, giving them instead freedom of civic and political action, without any 'benevolência ou favor' [benevolence or favour], so that they could obtain from the church 'formação cívico-político, de forma a tomarem plena consciência dos problemas da comunidade portuguesa, na concreta conjuntura presente, e estarem aptos a assumir as responsabilidades que lhes podem e devem caber' [civic and political education, so as to become fully aware of the problems facing the Portuguese community, in the present conjuncture, and be prepared to take on the responsibilities that could and should fall to them]. Although the prelate's reasoning did not give any hint as to the form that political activity by Catholics in general might take, he was driven by the concern to strengthen the alternative to Marxist forces. Following that logic, though, political participation by Catholics would involve considering the problem of the relation of the state with civil society, something that would go beyond the question of simply defending the interests of the church.[11]

The Government and the Political Management of the 'Bishop of Porto Case'

The impact of the Bishop of Porto's memorandum was due to the presentation made within it of an ecclesiastic and political vision that countered both the position of the church hierarchy, in relation to its stated position on the political activity of Catholics and on the institutional relationship of the church and state, and the Government's policy on social and political organization.

Salazar regarded the demand for political autonomy for Catholics within the framework of the regime, as presented by the Bishop of Porto, as a political assault on the *Estado Novo*. Jealous of the independence of the political authority in the face of civil society and the interests that appeared within it, he

[10] This declaration by D. António Ferreira Gomes may not have resulted simply from a doctrinal position, but may have been related also to the atmosphere of social and political agitation that had spread over the country in the post-electoral period. After the election there had been various strikes in political protest and other actions against the 'burla eleitoral' [electoral fraud], the majority of them organized by the Portuguese Communist Party (PCP), or in response to its provocations (Cf. *Avante!*, no. 257, 2nd fortnight of June 1958, and no. 280, September 1959; PT/TT/AOS/CO/PC-51: «As eleições foram falseadas», document of the Comissão Política do Comité Central do PCP, 18 June 1958).
[11] Cf. 'Pró-memória para uma entrevista' [text by D. António Ferreira Gomes, dated 13 July 1958, addressed to Salazar], in *D. António Ferreira Gomes nos 40 Anos da Carta do Bispo do Porto a Salazar* (Lisbon: Centro de Estudos de História Religiosa/ Multinova, 1998), pp. 175–92.

refused to accept that a member of the ecclesiastical hierarchy should be able to shelter behind the autonomy of the church from the state to discuss the state's options in matters of economic and social policy, and still less to object to the limitations placed on the civil liberties of its citizens. He also strongly objected to the prelate's departure from the principle that the church's role in politics should be exclusively limited to a defence of its own interests. It did not pass unnoticed by Salazar that the Bishop's position represented a rupture with the dominant position of the Portuguese episcopate over what the involvement of Catholics in political matters should be, involving as it did a claim for a larger space for Catholic intervention in society and a right to distance themselves from the regime. To Salazar, the Bishop of Porto was endorsing a specifically party-political activity by Catholics, opening up space for *Acão Católica* to transform itself into a political force in competition with the *União Nacional* and even to seek to take control of the apparatus of state.[12]

The prestige that D. António Ferreira Gomes enjoyed as an ecclesiastic, both as a noted intellectual and as the man responsible for one of the most important dioceses in Portugal, in both historical and pastoral terms, made the matter more serious. The fact that he gave repeated assurances that his views were strictly personal, and that he had not discussed them with the Patriarch of Lisbon or other bishops,[13] did not prevent them being seen as an institutional ecclesiastical position (the Bishop acknowledged as much in his memorandum), from which Salazar drew the conclusion that they had implications for the institutional relationship between the state and the Catholic Church. His reasoning on this point may have been due in part to his suspicions that the Holy See might have plans to promote a political transition in Portugal.[14]

Salazar's reaction to the 'Bishop of Porto Case' is understandable in the light of this perception. For him, the most important thing was to establish from the religious authorities to what extent the church (the Portuguese episcopate, and more particularly the Holy See) was interested in promoting political activity by means of the ACP, with the aim of forming a Christian political party. On the existence or not of such an intention amongst the religious authorities and of their admission or denial of the same would depend good institutional relations between the state and the Catholic Church, Salazar believed. He sought clarification particularly from the Vatican, rather than the Portuguese episcopate, meaning that the case had a strong diplomatic element. The choice of the Holy See as the Portuguese government's privileged interlocutor was made

[12]　Cf. letter from Salazar dated 18 September 1958, to the nuncio Fernando Cento; cited in Manuel Braga da Cruz, *O Estado Novo e a Igreja Católica* (Lisbon: Editorial Bizâncio, 1998), pp. 116–19.
[13]　Cf. Manuel de Pinho Ferreira, *A Igreja e o Estado Novo na obra de D. António Ferreira Gomes* (Porto: Universidade Católica Portuguesa/ Faculdade de Teologia, 2004), pp. 275–84; Bruno Cardoso Reis, *Salazar e o Vaticano* (Lisbon: Imprensa de Ciências Sociais, 2006), p. 272.
[14]　Cf. José Barreto, 'O caso do Bispo do Porto em arquivos do Estado', in *Profecia e Liberdade em D. António Ferreira Gomes: atas do simpósio*, ed. by Paulo Bernardino (Lisbon: Ajuda à Igreja que Sofre, 2000), pp. 119–45.

not only for reasons of internal church hierarchies, but because, in Salazar's eyes, it was necessary to ascertain the Vatican's real intentions regarding the Portuguese political situation. In fact, Salazar viewed the possibility of the Holy See getting involved in a project for Christian Democracy as the greater threat.[15]

During the whole time, Salazar never succeeding in obtaining any more on the question of the nature of the ACP than a confirmation of the habitual papal doctrine. Furthermore, his attention was called to the fact that the ACP, in its official documents, had never transgressed the norm of 'estar fora e acima dos partidos' [being outside and above political parties].[16] Salazar was also dissatisfied with declarations by Cardinal Cerejeira, on the opening of the Jubilee Year of Catholic Action, on 16 November 1958, which gave assurances that '[a] organização não é um partido politico, nem sequer o germe dum partido' [the organization is neither a political party, nor even the germ of a party], but 'um movimento temporal de ação social' [a lay movement for social action]. The Patriarch of Lisbon would use the occasion to publicly clarify the relationship between the ACP and the political participation of its affiliates. Replying indirectly to the question of the possible formation a Christian Democratic party in Portugal, cherished by elements of the ACP, or of the organization itself turning into such a party, the Cardinal insisted that 'a Ação Católica não poderia nunca identificar-se com um partido democrata-cristão, por exemplo, se ele existisse' [Ação Católica could never identify itself with a Christian Democratic party, for example, if such a party existed]. All that was required of Christians and the 'ação social da Ação Católica' [social action of Ação Católica] was 'cristianizar as instituições da vida social fazendo passer nelas o espírito cristão' [to Christianize the institutions of social life, by bringing to them the Christian spirit], in as much as there was 'lugar e necessidade' [a place and a need].[17]

Salazar's dissatisfaction with these declarations was due not so much to the doctrine outlined by the Patriarch of Lisbon as to the way in which he had chosen to approach the question. Despite the personal authority of the Patriarch and the moment chosen to deal with the question of the ACP's operation, Salazar would have preferred a collective statement on the issue from the episcopate, explicitly distancing themselves from the ideas elaborated by the Bishop of Porto in his memorandum.[18] In the face of the religious authorities'

[15] Cf. letter from Salazar, dated 18 September 1958, sent to the nuncio Fernando Cento; cited in Manuel Braga da Cruz, ibidem, pp. 118–19.
[16] Cf. Note from the Vatican Secretary of State, dated 2 October 1958, cited in Manuel Braga da Cruz, ibidem, p. 120; letter from the apostolic nuncio, Fernando Cento, to Salazar, dated 7 December 1958, cited by Manuel Braga da Cruz, ibidem, pp. 127–28; PT/TT/AOS/CO/PC-52: information from Ramiro Valadão, supplied to the ministro da Presidência, Pedro Teotónio Pereira, dated 15 January 1959.
[17] Cf. D. Manuel Gonçalves Cerejeira, 'A natureza da Ação Católica', in Obras Pastorais, vol. V (Lisbon: União Gráfica, 1960), pp. 289–93.
[18] Cf. letter from Salazar to the apostolic nuncio, dated 6 December 1958; cited by Manuel Braga da Cruz, ibidem, p. 125.

behaviour, Salazar hardened his position on the state's attitude towards the ecclesiastical institutions, opting for two forms of pressure: first, by reminding the Holy See, in diplomatic correspondence, that it was unclear if the ACP was protected by Article III of the Concordat, which could leave it open for the Executive to withdraw its tolerance towards the organization and demand its closure;[19] and second, by declaring in a public speech on the occasion of the taking of office of the new Executive Commission of the *União Nacional* that the involvement of Catholics in electoral and post-electoral periods could put in question the terms of the Concordat and the institutional relations between the state and the church.[20] In this way Salazar avoided making direct reference to matters involving the Bishop of Porto, but it was clear that this episode was the most serious for relations between the state and the church in that period, so there was no doubt that it was that case, in particular, that was commanding Salazar's attention.

Salazar's tactics, while unwelcome, did not lead the religious authorities to say anything really new about the ACP, or about the institutional relationship between the church and the state.[21] Neither the Portuguese episcopate nor the Holy See was inclined to make any public pronouncement to censure or distance themselves from the doctrinal position that D. António Ferreira Gomes had taken on the ACP in this memorandum, which they chose to regard as a purely personal pronouncement. This response corresponded to an intention to avoid the possible conflict inherent in the case: by not taking the Bishop's position as institutional, the religious authorities made it more difficult for the government to draw from it formal consequences regarding the relationship between church and state. In a pastoral letter dated 16 January 1959 the Portuguese bishops would highlight the relations of 'independência e cooperação' [independence and cooperation] that they had been maintaining with the civil authorities, and would confirm the church's essential doctrine on *Ação Católica*, emphasizing that that organization could not 'identificar-se com um partido politico, nem a sua ação com uma ação política' [identify itself as a political party, nor its activity with political activity], since 'diferentes os fins, o objeto e os meios de ação' [their aims, objective and methods of operation were different]. By way of this episcopal document, the prelates sought to reject the accusations that the church in Portugal was 'enfeudada à Situação política' [subordinated to the political establishment], saying that, in those circumstances, 'a Hierarquia trairia a autoridade divina de que está revestida pondo-se ao service daquilo para que não a recebeu' [the Hierarchy would be betraying the divine authority invested

---

[19] cf. Idem, *ibidem*.

[20] Cf. António de Oliveira Salazar, 'Na posse da Comissão Executiva da União Nacional' [speech given on 6 December 1958, at the headquarters of the *União Nacional*], in *Discursos e Notas Políticas*, vol. V (1951–1958), (Coimbra: Coimbra Editora, 1959), pp. 516–17.

[21] Cf. letter from the apostolic nuncio, Monsignor Fernando Cento, to Salazar, dated 7 December 1958, cited in Bruno Cardoso Reis, *ibidem*, p. 269, PT/TT/AOS/CD — 10, fls. 101–06; letter from José Nosolini to Salazar, sent from the Portuguese Embassy in Madrid, dated 25 December 1958.

in it by placing itself at the service of a purpose for which it did not receive it].
As for Catholics, specifically in their 'ação política e social' [social and political
activity] they affirmed that 'são livres e é da sua inteira responsabilidade a
opção concreta tomada, se bem que católicas não representam a igreja' [they are
free [agents] and the concrete choice made is entirely their responsibility, since
Catholics do not represent the church].[22]

Salazar could not then claim a victory, as he would have liked, with the
publication of this episcopal document. It was true that the pastoral letter did
clarify that the church's institutional relationship with the regime remained
unchanged, continuing along the same lines as those established at the time
of the Concordat, and that the religious authorities were not encouraging
Catholics to engage in specifically party political activity, least of all by way of
the ACP. However, it was obvious that the document confirmed the formal unity
amongst the bishops (since D. António signed it too), and in no way criticized
or distanced itself from the Bishop of Porto, as Salazar had clearly expected of
the religious authorities. This was not an insignificant aspect, as it encapsulated
the problem of the head of government's political authority, as he himself
understood it: his leadership had been weakened by the Bishop of Porto, who
had offended him by putting forward in his memorandum positions contrary
to those of the state on the political participation of Catholics, by making use
of 'privilégios da Concordata para exercer ação política' [the privileges of the
Concordat to engage in political activity], and had thereby strengthened the
political struggle in various sections of society against the regime. It would
have been this matter, that had been in dispute since August 1958, that Salazar
would attempt to resolve by concentrating his efforts on removing D. António
from the diocese of Porto, immediately after the publication of the bishops'
pastoral letter.

In fact Salazar would abandon the plan that he had first fixed upon, of
requesting explanations at the highest level, settling instead on a plan firmly
based on internal politics. He set out to demonstrate that the political authority
would not tolerate affronts, wherever they came from, and that he would act
to restore 'ordem pública' [public order], by seeking in this case, as in any
other, the appropriate punishment for a citizen who had undermined political
authority. For Salazar, naturally, the fact that D. António was a bishop made
the matter worse. In his view, the Bishop of Porto had made an 'ataque político'
[political attack] on the government, which had made 'incompatível com o
Estado a sua presença à frente da diocese do Porto' [his position at the head of
the Porto diocese irreconcilable with the state].[23] This point was not pursued
by Salazar in his diplomatic contacts with the Holy See, but was included in the

---

[22]   Cf. 'Pastoral coletiva do episcopado metropolitano' [dated 16 January 1959], in *Brotéria*, vol.
LXVIII, n.º 2, February 1959, pp. 202–09.
[23]   Cf. Telegram from the Minister for Foreign Affairs, dated 31 January 1959, addressed to the
Portuguese Ambassador to the Holy See, cited by Manuel Braga da Cruz, *ibidem*, p. 129

instructions given to the Portuguese ambassador to the Vatican, right from the beginning of discussions.[24]

In his approach to the problem, Salazar wished to avoid acting without seeking some support from the Holy See. He was aware that to remove the Bishop of Porto by purely governmental means would create serious problems, and could even lead to a rupture between the state and the Holy See and the episcopate, as well as a very predictable discord with various sectors of Catholic society forming part of the social base that supported the regime. Salazar foresaw that in that event Catholics would overcome their differences and form themselves into a bloc against the government, and would also be able to count on the support of the opposition to the regime.[25] It should be added that the Concordat and the constitutional separation of church and state would weigh against the legitimacy of any direct intervention by the Executive to suspend or to remove D. António, since that would be seen as a formal violation of ecclesiastical freedom and of the principles of church doctrine and canon law.

Between January and June 1959, through numerous contacts between Portuguese diplomats and the Vatican, the Portuguese government therefore put pressure on the Holy See to remove the bishop from his diocese, and not to allow him to take over the running of any other diocese, even. To this end it was argued that the pastoral letter issued by the prelates on 19 January exposed the doctrinal and pastoral contradictions between the bishops' official position and the position that D. António had adopted in his memorandum, and that it could not be expected that the state could establish a cooperative relationship with him, nor with an ecclesiastical hierarchy that gave cover to the pastoral and doctrinal positions of one of its members, even when these clashed with the political principles of the regime. In his understanding, the whole business set a bad example, which could lead to other bishops also taking positions that were equally unhelpful for the institutional relationships between the religious authorities and the state.[26] He also argued that the case could continue to provoke a climate of social agitation and political challenges to the political authorities, leading to even deeper ecclesiastical divisions. These might also affect organizations of the ACP, despite several pastoral interventions by Cardinal Cerejeira on the political stance of activists, elements of whom continued to demand freedom of political organization for Catholics and wider political freedoms in general.[27]

---

[24] Cf. Letter from the apostolic nuncio, dated 6 December 1958; order from Salazar, date 18 September 1958; and telegram from the Minister for Foreign Affairs, dated 20 November 1958, addressed to the Portuguese Ambassador to the Holy See, cited by Manuel Braga da Cruz, *ibidem*, p. 121 and p. 126.

[25] Cf. PT/TT/AOS/CO/PC-51: copy of telegram no. 41 sent by Salazar to the Portuguese Ambassador to the Vatican, on 14 April 1959.

[26] Cf. Telegram from the Minister for Foreign Affairs to the Portuguese Ambassador to the Vatican, dated 5 February 1959, cited by Manuel Braga da Cruz, *ibidem*, pp. 133–34.

[27] Cf. PT/TT/AOS/CO/PC-51: copy of telegram no. 41 sent by Salazar to the Portuguese Ambassador to the Vatican, on 14 April 1959; PT/TT/AOS/CO/PC — 51: copy of a statement by twenty-seven padres from the Lisbon diocese, dated 23 April 1959; *Novidades*, 5 June 1959, p. 1.

The inflexibility in the Portuguese position and a fear that the government might even denounce the Concordat, along with an increase in tension within the church over the case, led the Holy See to make a discreet approach on the subject, suggesting that the Bishop might leave the country for a while to allow passions to calm down.[28] From the Vatican's point of view such a departure would be merely temporary and there was an expectation that the Executive would quickly forget the episode, but this calculation seemed to have ignored Salazar's warning that once D. António left Portugal he would not be allowed to return.[29] In fact the Bishop of Porto would leave the country as advised on 24 July 1959. However, when he later attempted to return to Portugal he was prevented from crossing the frontier by the civil authorities, and spent ten years in exile. But despite having succeeded in getting D. António removed from his diocese, the Executive did not approve of the way that the Vatican had handled the case, nor did it welcome the nomination of an apostolic administrator for the diocese (the Vatican's choice for the job fell on D. Florentino de Andrade e Silva), especially since the appointment was regarded as of 'carácter excecional' [an exceptional character]. For this reason Portuguese diplomacy in the years following continued to demand that D. António Ferreira Gomes should be definitively removed from his diocese.[30]

Political Effects of the Bishop of Porto Case

Right up to the end of his period of government, Salazar always tried to emphasize in his public pronouncements on the relationship between church and state that the cooperative relationship between the civil power and the religious authorities had not been damaged by the 'Bishop of Porto case'. As regards the separation of church and state, he always maintained that the terms of the Concordat of 1940 had been respected. The Concordat itself and the preferential treatment given by the institution of the state to the Catholic Church remained in force.[31] However, he still refused to allow the regime to take on an overtly confessional character, as some elements within Catholicism would have liked. The occasion of the constitutional revision of 1959 was illustrative of the resistance of the Executive to those interests. At a time when he was politically weak and when the 'Bishop of Porto case' was damaging the image of the government amongst various sections of Catholic opinion who

[28]   The Holy See would choose for this mission the titular Patriarch of the Indies, D. José da Costa Nunes, who was charged with making an apostolic visit to the diocese of Porto (Cf. Bruno Cardoso Reis, *ibidem*, pp. 282–83).

[29]   Cf. Confidential report of a conversation between Salazar and the Patriarch of the Indies, dated 18 June 1959; telegram from the Minister for Foreign Affairs to the Portuguese Ambassador to the Holy See, dated 9 March 1959, cited by Manuel Braga da Cruz, *ibidem*, pp. 140 and 142.

[30]   Cf. Bruno Cardoso Reis, *ibidem*, pp. 288–93.

[31]   Cf. António de Oliveira Salazar, *Entrevistas (1960–1966)* (Coimbra: Coimbra Editora, 1967), pp. 16–18, 173–74.

were critical of the regime, Salazar could have bolstered his support amongst broad circles of Catholics by agreeing to introduce the name of God into the constitution. However, he opted to avoid damaging the balance of interests that supported the regime by not favouring Catholic interests to the detriment of the interests of currents of lay sensibility which formed part of his social base of support.[32] By the end of his time as prime minister Salazar agreed to hand over land in the possession of the state to the Patriarch of Lisbon for the construction in that city of the Universidade Católica, and proceeded with the publication of some legislation favourable to particular activities undertaken by the church, including the following: the Estatuto da Saúde e Assistência [Statute of Health and Social Assistance], in 1963; official recognition for elementary primary education provided by Catholic missions in Portugal, granted in 1964; the regulation of moral and religious education to be provided in official primary schools, in 1965; and the creation, in 1966, of a permanent religious support service for the armed forces.[33] The last two measures required negotiations with the Holy See, given that they involved matters that fell within the ambit of the Concordat on 1940, but had not yet been transposed into Portuguese civil law. Such cooperative dealings between the Portuguese government and the Vatican authorities indicate that the tensions that had been evident in the course of the events surrounding D. António Ferreira Gomes were gradually being overcome, as they attempted to secure negotiations over other matters. Also pertinent to overcoming those tensions between the two parties was the policy that Pope John XXIII commended to the universal church for keeping the clergy out of politics.[34] Throughout the 1960s and up until 1974, new rifts would appear between the Portuguese government and the Vatican authorities; however, those conflicts should not be regarded as vestiges of the 'Bishop of Porto case', being associated rather with the colonial policy followed by Portugal, which the Holy See regarded at intractable. During those years the Vatican would develop a policy of creating autochthonous and autonomous bishoprics in Portuguese Africa (Angola and Mozambique), sympathetic to recognizing the rights of native peoples to self-determination, and hence to the movement towards independence for the colonial territories.[35]

Compared to the relationship with the Holy See, that between Salazar and the metropolitan episcopate and the majority of Portuguese bishops overseas was more consensual and subject to less distrust, as can be seen from the

[32]   Cf. Paula Borges Santos, *A Questão Religiosa no Parlamento (1935-1974)*, Vol. III (Lisbon: Assembleia da República, 2011), pp. 126–32.
[33]   Cf. Paula Borges Santos, 'A Política Religiosa do Estado Novo (1933–1974): Estado, Leis, Governação e Interesses Religiosos...', pp. 341–48.
[34]   Cf. Bruno Cardoso Reis, *ibidem*, pp. 302–04. The author demonstrates that John XXIII, while recognizing that the Portuguese regime allowed only limited civic liberties, nevertheless censured the behaviour of the Bishop of Porto on account of what he considered his 'insensato' [senseless] involvement in matters of national politics.
[35]   Cf. Paula Borges Santos, *Igreja Católica, Estado e Sociedade (1968-1975): o caso Rádio Renascença* (Lisbon: Imprensa de Ciências Sociais, 2005), pp. 91–93.

correspondence exchanged between them. The Executive always made an appearance in official religious ceremonies.[36] Even in the midst of the conflict with the Bishop of Porto, Salazar received and dealt with critical remarks from other bishops, although these related exclusively to aspects of the so-called 'matérias mistas' [mixed forum], and did not involve political matters.[37] Later Salazar acceded to some requests from various prelates, some involving the return of ecclesiastical properties.[38] The climate of reconciliation between the civil power and the Portuguese bishops became evident in the manifestations of solidarity with Salazar that some members of the ecclesiastical hierarchy chose to make on the occasion of the hijacking of the *Santa Maria* (January 1961), the invasion of Goa by the Indian government (1961), and the start of the wars in Africa.[39]

The way that Salazar handled the 'Bishop of Porto case' had consequences for the relationship between the government and those Catholics who were critical of the government. Salazar's strategy seems to have had two prongs: the first, the crystallization of the principle that there should be no political organization of Catholics, closing off the possibility of their making an organized political intervention in the manner of the *União Nacional*; and the second, to strengthen the mechanisms of state repression to control and contain those elements who were creating 'alta tensão' [heightened tension] against the civil powers.

[36] Cf. PT/TT/AOS/CP — 15, Pt. 22, fls. 367, 371 and 372: official notes of thanks from the Archbishop of Mytilene, D. Manuel dos Santos Rocha, to Salazar, dated 6 November 1960, 14 June 1963 and 10 July 1963.
[37] The fiercest criticism of the political establishment was made in August 1958, by the Bishop of Bragança and Miranda, D. Abílio Vaz das Neves, who protested vehemently to the prime minister about the place given to private confessional education in the educational system and to the time devoted to religious instruction in the public school system. The Bishop's letter is significant because it encapsulates the sense of dissatisfaction amongst Catholics about the provisions of the 1933 Constitution and of the Concordat of 1940 concerning instruction and schooling, and it also summarizes the principal Catholic demands in the field of education, as they appeared throughout the length of the regime. Salazar's response, made months later, reveals a certain capacity for dialogue with the ecclesiastical hierarchy over the criticisms, which centred on matters related to the so-called 'interesses históricos' [historical interests] of the religious establishment and which were made discreetly, without becoming public knowledge. It seems important to emphasize this response by Salazar and to see it as counterpoint to the political response that he gave chose to give to D. António Ferreira Gomes. (Cf. PT/TT/AOS/CP-33, Pt. 1, fls. 413–14: letter from D. Abílio Vaz das Neves to Salazar, dated 28 August 1958; PT/TT/AOS/CP-33, Pt. 1, fls. 423–28: letter from Salazar to the Bishop of Bragança and Miranda, dated 10 January 1959).
[38] Cf. PT/TT/AOS/CP — 15, Pt. 1, fls. 207–09, 213: letters from D. Francisco Rendeiro to Salazar, dated 28 April 1962 and 9 January 1963; official reply by Salazar to the Bishop of the Algarve, dated 12 January 1963; *Diário do Governo*, I Série, n.º 33: Decreto-Lei n.º 44 875, 8 February 1963; *Diário do Governo*, I Série, n.º 290: Decreto-Lei n.º 45 423, 11 December 1963; *Diário do Governo*, I Série, n.º 195: Decreto-Lei n.º 47 159, 23 August 1966; *Diário do Governo*, I Série, n.º 101: Decreto-Lei n.º 48 356, 27 April 1968.
[39] Cf. PT/TT/AOS/CP-33, fls. 83, 131 and 317: telegram from the Archbishop of Évora to Salazar, dated 18 December 1961; telegram from Archbishop/Bishop of Coimbra to Salazar, dated 23 December 1961; telegram from the Bishop of Porto Amélia to Salazar, dated December; PT/TT/AOS/CP-33, fls. 282: card from the Bishop of Portalegre and Castelo Branco to Salazar, dated 16 March 1961; PT/TT/AOS/CP-33, fls. 221, 231, 292, 343: telegram from the Bishop of Leiria to Salazar, dated 27 August 1963; telegram from the Bishop of Luso to Salazar, undated; letter from the Bishop of Portalegre and Castelo Branco to Salazar, dated 9 August 1962; card from the Bishop of Vila Cabral to Salazar, dated 3 December 1967.

The first strategy was informed by Salazar's continuing belief that a Catholic political party was only useful for the 'defesa no campo político da comunidade religiosa' [defence in the political sphere of the religious community], when it was 'ignorada pelo Poder, escravizada pelas leis, posta à margem da liberdade corrente' [ignored by the political authority, enslaved by its laws, pushed to the margins of normal liberties].[40] From Salazar's statements we may conclude, in part by regarding specifically party-political activity by Catholics in the light of the conditions that justified the creation of the CCP, that he doubted that in a regime such as the *Estado Novo* it was necessary for Catholics to defend their church by way of a Catholic political party, especially since the government had an institutional cooperative relationship with the church, consolidated through the Concordat, which allowed it to occupy a 'situação de privilégio' [privileged position].

The second strategy was a response to the growing dissatisfaction with government policies, which from 1958 onwards was prevalent not only in opposition circles by also within elements of those political forces which supported the government. Salazar blamed the ecclesiastical hierarchy for the behaviour of Catholic elements that he perceived as undermining public order and of resisting or opposing the regime. This reading of the situation, that there was a problem of indiscipline in the Catholic camp that the religious authorities were failing to control, served in part as a justification for state repression. The state would intervene where the ecclesiastical authorities could not secure the necessary respect for the constituted government, and such action would, it was asserted, avoid further harm to the relationship between church and state.[41] From the 1960s onwards the regime sought to restrain any civic activity by Catholics that encompassed a reaction against the political authorities or demanded the right to intervene in society, by exercising greater socio-political responsibilities of through associations, trade unions or political parties. This involved greater vigilance by the political police (the PIDE) over the activities of lay activists, Catholic priests and some bishops suspected of disaffection from the regime, not only in the metropolis but also in the colonies. As well as gathering information about the political activities of many Catholics, the PIDE also made politically motivated arrests of a number of lay activists and priests.[42]

---

[40]   Excerpts from an interview given by Salazar to the *Corriere della Sera*, 30 March 1960, transcribed and translated in António de Oliveira Salazar, *Entrevistas (1960–1966)...*, 1967, pp. 17–18.

[41]   Cf. Paula Borges Santos, 'A Politica Religiosa do Estado Novo', pp. 364–72.

[42]   Cf. José Barreto, *Religião e Sociedade: dois ensaios* (Lisbon: Imprensa de Ciências Sociais, 2002), pp. 125–26; João Miguel Almeida, *A oposição católica ao Estado Novo (1958–1974)* (Lisbon: Edições Nelson de Matos, 2008), pp. 126, 145–46, 226.

Conclusion

Contrary to Salazar's fears, no confessional party appeared in Portugal at any time up to the end of the authoritarian regime in April 1974. Nor were his suspicions confirmed that some religious authorities, whether in the Vatican or in Portugal, were trying to promote political activity by the ACP, with the intention of fomenting a political transition to a pluralist democracy, which would involve creating a political party of a Christian Democratic orientation. In fact, during the whole time that Cardinal Cerejeira was Patriarch (1929–71) the Portuguese bishops refrained from specifically party-political activities, while the belief that Catholics enjoyed individual freedom of political activity remained closely linked to the principle that Catholics should defend the interests of the church in public life, and inspire the policies and the agenda of the government in particular. Only in 1973, during the patriarchate of D. António Ribeiro, did the bishops show any inclination to confer religious legitimacy on the support for political pluralism that existed in the Catholic camp, based on recognizing the existence amongst Christians of differing opinions on the type of representation and participation regarded as adequate for an intervention into society.

However, coming late as it did, this evolution in the thinking amongst the ecclesiastical hierarchy was seen to be insufficient to meet the aspirations of various sectors of Catholic opinion for political participation. Under the influence of the Second Vatican Council, some Christians reformulated their notion of political activity, abandoning the focus on defence of the *libertas ecclesiae* and contesting in particular any ideology that insisted on the exclusion of religion from the public sphere or permitted its presence only under the close supervision of the state. From the mid-1960s the notion of political activity for many Catholics came to be centred on the protection of certain personal rights in public life (such as the right of assembly, freedom of association, freedom of expression and religious freedom), on the restructuring of relations of citizens between themselves and with the public authorities (censuring some political practices that restricted civil and religious liberties and denouncing some abuses of power harmful to the rights of individuals). It was also within this trajectory that certain sectors of Catholic opinion started to contest the colonial wars that the government was engaged in, from 1961, in Angola, Mozambique and Guiné. They also insisted that the institutions of the church could in no way be confused with the political system or remain subordinate to the civil authorities by virtue of the privileges they had secured.

These changes in Catholic thinking about these new problems came to their maturity during the 'consulate' of Marcelo Caetano, who took over the position of *Presidente do Conselho* [prime minister] in 1968. However, despite operating in a swiftly changing political and ecclesiastical environment, Caetano maintained Salazar's strategy of rejecting plural political parties and even intensified the repression directed against Catholic opinion hostile to the regime, introducing prior censorship of the publications of the ACP for the first time. This move was ineffective, taking place in an unhealthy climate of conflict between the political authorities and Catholic opinion. It not only increased Catholic hostility towards the regime, but also contributed to the government closing in upon itself.

Translated from Portuguese by Richard Correll

Abstracts

The Unmappable Sertão

Rex P. Nielson

Abstract. This article traces the intellectual history of the *sertão* as a concept that not only signifies distinct geographical and topographical traits but also Portugal's projection of cultural Otherness. Though the *sertão* remains inextricably bound to Brazilian culture, this article seeks to demonstrate the Portuguese roots of the *sertão*, especially as manifest in Portuguese cartography from the sixteenth to the nineteenth centuries. The cartographic history of the *sertão* deepens our understanding of Portugal's cartographic imagination, colonial expansion, exploration of Brazil's vast interior, and encounters with indigenous peoples.
Keywords. Sertão, cartography, maps, Brazil, Portugal, otherness.

Resumo. Este artigo investiga a história intelectual do sertão como um conceito que não apenas contém atributos geográficos e topográficos distintos mas também a projeção portuguesa de alteridade cultural. Embora o sertão permaneça hoje inseparável da cultura brasileira, este artigo demonstra as raízes portuguesas do sertão, sobretudo como são manifestadas na cartografia portuguesa do século XVI até o século XIX. A história cartográfica do sertão aprofunda nossa compreensão da imaginação cartográfica de Portugal, como também a expansão colonial, a exploração do vasto interior do Brasil e os encontros com povos indígenas.
Palavras-chave. Sertão, cartografia, mapas, Brasil, Portugal, alteridade.

A Poetry of Flesh and Bone: Miguel de Unamuno and Miguel Torga

Robert Patrick Newcomb

Abstract. This article looks to the figure of 'flesh and bone' to compare the poetry of Miguel de Unamuno, from Spain, and Miguel Torga, from Portugal. I focus on three biblical connotations of 'flesh and bone' to be observed in the two poets: *filiation, concreteness,* and *mutual dependence.* I argue that Unamuno and Torga's variegated usage of 'flesh and bone' works to centre their poetry on those individuals that Unamuno, who decisively influenced Torga, termed 'men of flesh and bone'. Further, I speak to the marked presence of biblical and more broadly religious imagery and language in the work of the two poets, who both maintained a conflicted, agonic attitude toward God.
Keywords. Miguel de Unamuno, Miguel Torga, flesh, bone, Iberianism, Bible.

Portuguese Studies vol. 30 no. 1 (2014), 112–16
© Modern Humanities Research Association 2014

RESUMO. No presente artigo, utilizamos a figura de 'carne e osso' para comparar a poesia de Miguel de Unamuno, de Espanha, e Miguel Torga, de Portugal. Analisamos três conotações bíblicas de 'carne e osso' que são patentes na obra dos dois poetas: *filiação*, *concretude*, e *dependência mútua*. Argumentamos que o uso variado de 'carne e osso' por Unamuno e Torga aponta para a centralidade dos que Unamuno, que teve uma influência decisiva sobre Torga, chamou de 'homens e carne e osso'. Também refletimos sobre a marcada presença de imagens e linguagem bíblicas e religiosas na obra dos dois poetas, cuja relação com Deus se caracterizou como conflituosa e agónica.
PALAVRAS-CHAVE. Miguel de Unamuno, Miguel Torga, carne, osso, iberismo, Bíblia.

The Mariquinhas Cycle: An Ongoing Saga of Prostitution, Changing Values in Lisbon and Spleen for an Undefined Past

MICHAEL COLVIN

ABSTRACT. This article examines the legend of fictitious Lisbon prostitute, Mariquinhas, who appears first in Alfredo Marceneiro and Silva Tavares's Fado ballad, 'A Casa da Mariquinhas', and subsequently in eleven songs that narrate her fate and that of her brothel. Whereas the Câmara Municipal de Lisboa begins to demolish the Capital's historic centre for the sake of urban renewal projects in the 1930s, many of the later Fados in the cycle are reset in threatened neighbourhoods and thus serve to denounce changing traditions in the face of progress. The leitmotif of the shuttered windows that links all of the songs in the cycle returns us to Marceneiro's original ballad, in which the wooden curtains kept the nosy neighbours from peeking in, and when the house itself — and Lisbon — was happier.
KEYWORDS. Fado, Lisbon, prostitution, Estado Novo, architecture, urban studies, Alfredo Marceneiro, Silva Tavares, Mariquinhas.

RESUMO. Este artigo examina a lenda da prostituta fictícia, Mariquinhas, que aparece pela primeira vez na balada de Alfredo Marceneiro e Silva Tavares, 'A Casa da Mariquinhas', e depois em onze fados que narram o destino dela e o do seu prostíbulo. Como a Câmara Municipal de Lisboa começa a demolir o centro histórico da capital em prol de reabilitação urbana a partir dos anos de 1930, muitos dos fados posteriores têm lugar nos bairros ameaçados, e assim servem para denunciar a perda de tradições por amor do progresso. O leitmotiv das janelas com tabuinhas que liga todas as canções no ciclo devolve-nos à balada original do Marceneiro em que as cortinas de madeira impediam as vizinhas coscuvilheiras de verem 'o que lá se passa' e quando as casas — e também Lisboa — eram mais felizes.
PALAVRAS-CHAVE. Fado, Lisboa, prostituição, Estado Novo, arquitetura, estudos urbanos, Alfredo Marceneiro, Silva Tavares, Mariquinhas.

Acção Realista Portuguesa: An Organization of the Anti-Liberal Right, 1923–26

Ernesto Castro Leal

ABSTRACT. This article sets out to analyse the milestones in the political and social ideology and the public activity of *Acção Realista Portuguesa*. This was an organization of the anti-liberal right, led by the intellectual Alfredo Pimenta, contributing to the diversity of the world of Portuguese nationalism. Between 1923 and 1926 it embodied a strand of anti-liberal, integralist monarchism — Integral Nationalism — that retained dynastic loyalty to D. Manuel II. This doctrinal strand of nationalism promoted a political ideology based on a traditional monarchy, with a King who would govern and choose his ministers, and with Estates General representative 'of the Church, of the Land, of the Intelligentsia, and of Production', and a social ideology based on organic corporativism (the family, the municipality and the professional syndicate). They were willing to contemplate, as a temporary measure, a military dictatorship, in order to defeat the existing regime of republican liberal democracy.

KEYWORDS. Portugal, *Acção Realista Portuguesa*, Alfredo Pimenta, authoritarianism, anti-liberalism, the political right.

RESUMO. Pretende-se analisar, neste artigo, marcos da ideologia político-social e da dinâmica pública da Acção Realista Portuguesa. Foi uma organização de direita antiliberal, liderada pelo intelectual Alfredo Pimenta, e contribuiu para a diversidade do universo nacionalista português. Entre 1923 e 1926, deu corpo a uma proposta de monarquismo integralista antiliberal — Nacionalismo Integral — , que manteve a obediência dinástica a Dom Manuel II. A doutrina deste nacionalismo promovia o ideário político da monarquia tradicional, com um Rei que governasse e escolhesse os ministros e com Cortes Gerais representativas 'da Igreja, da Terra, da Inteligência e da Produção', e o ideário social do corporativismo orgânico (família, município e sindicato profissional). Admitiram, transitoriamente, um regime político de ditadura militar, para superar o regime político demoliberal republicano.

PALAVRAS-CHAVE. Portugal, Alfredo Pimenta, política, autoritarismo, antiliberalismo, direita.

The Integralism of Plínio Salgado: Luso-Brazilian Relations

Leandro Pereira Gonçalves

ABSTRACT. This article aims to investigate the path followed by Plínio Salgado in the formation and development of Brazilian Integralism. While drawing on many currents, it set out to build an original political doctrine. However, the ideas in circulation at the time influenced its leader considerably in the formation of his thought. From Portugal, he had the doctrinaire example of Lusitanian Integralism, a movement of an extreme right-wing nationalist character whose formation was clearly based on *Action Française*, the forerunner of conservatism which, like all the political groups of the early twentieth century, elaborated a practical response to the ideas proposed by Pope Leo XIII in 1891, through the *Rerum Novarum*. This article is based on the concept of political culture and aims to analyse the thought of the Integralist leader, while focusing on the context of the Lusitanian influence and the essentially Catholic precept that accompanied him throughout his life.

KEYWORDS. Plínio Salgado, Lusitanian Integralism, Radical Conservatism, Brazil-Portugal.

RESUMO. Este ensaio tem como objetivo a investigação da trajetória de Plínio Salgado na formação e desenvolvimento do integralismo brasileiro. Com matrizes múltiplas tinha como propósito a construção de uma doutrina política original. No entanto a circulação de ideias fez com que o seu leader sofresse influências consideráveis na formação de seu pensamento. De Portugal recebeu o exemplo doutrinário do Integralismo Lusitano, um movimento da direita radical nacionalista inspirada pela *Action Française*, formação precursora de grupos conservadores do princípio do século XX que estabeleceram uma resposta prática à teoria proferida pelo Papa Leão XIII, em 1891, através da *Rerum Novarum*. Com base no conceito de cultura política, o artigo propõe a análise do pensamento do líder integralista centrada no contexto de influência lusitana e preceito basicamente católico que o acompanhou toda a vida.

PALAVRAS-CHAVE. Plínio Salgado, Integralismo Lusitano, Conservadorismo Radical, Brasil-Portugal.

The Question of the Political Organization of Catholics under the Portuguese Authoritarian Regime: The 'Bishop of Porto Case' (1958)

PAULA BORGES SANTOS

ABSTRACT. A significant aspect of the Portuguese authoritarian regime was its refusal to allow the organization of plural political parties, and the government was seen to be vigilant towards any organizations, activities or tendencies that might favour organized political intervention by Catholics, outside the single party system. The authorities' policy of countering signs of political autonomy in the public arena amongst Catholics was strengthened in 1958 when Salazar came into conflict with the Bishop of Porto, who demanded freedom of political organization for Catholics. That conflict is discussed here, since it was the event that created the greatest tension between the Catholic Church and the state during the course of the Salazar regime. The article examines how the government handled the case, and analyses its political effects on relations between the civil powers and the religious authorities and with groups of Catholics who were critical towards the regime.

KEYWORDS. Portugal, Catholic Church, Salazar, D. António Ferreira Gomes, Catholic party, Christian democracy.

RESUMO. Da ideologia do regime autoritário português fez parte a recusa do pluralismo partidário. O Governo mostrou-se sempre vigilante perante organizações, ações ou dinâmicas que pudessem favorecer uma intervenção politicamente organizada dos católicos, fora do sistema de partido único. A estratégia do poder político de desmobilização de manifestações de autonomia política dos católicos na esfera pública foi reforçada em 1958, quando Salazar entrou em conflito com o bispo do Porto, que reclamava liberdade de organização política para os católicos. Acompanha-se aqui esse conflito, por ser aquele que, relacionado com a questão da participação política dos católicos, maior tensão trouxe, durante o salazarismo, às relações do Estado com a Igreja Católica. Caracteriza-se a gestão política que o Governo fez do caso e analisam-se os seus efeitos políticos, nas relações do poder civil com as autoridades religiosas e com setores católicos críticos do regime.

PALAVRAS-CHAVE. Portugal, Igreja Católica, Salazar, D. António Ferreira Gomes, partido católico, democracia-cristã.

www.ingramcontent.com/pod-product-compliance
Lightning Source LLC
Chambersburg PA
CBHW050525280326
41932CB00014B/2464